BREAK THE CYCLE, NOT YOURSELF

A Conscious Mother's Guide to Breaking
Generational Patterns Without Losing Yourself

ALICIA BROWN, MS., LMFT

Copyright © 2025 Alicia Brown

All rights reserved.

ISBN: 978-1-83556-421-9

No part of this book may be used or reproduced, distributed, or transmitted in any manner whatsoever without written permission from the author or publisher, except as permitted by U.S. copyright law. For permission requests, speaking inquiries, and bulk order purchase options, please contact: alicia@nurturedconnections.com

This book is not intended to replace the advice of or treatment by other health-care professionals. It should be considered an additional resource only. Questions and concerns about mental or physical health should always be discussed with a doctor or other health-care professional.

The author and publisher make no representations or warranties of any kind and shall not be held liable for any loss or damage alleged to be caused directly or indirectly by the information contained in this book. Readers are encouraged to always seek professional support when needed.

All names and identifying details in this book have been changed or omitted to protect the privacy and confidentiality of individuals. Some stories are composites drawn from multiple experiences to illustrate key themes, preserve anonymity, and uphold ethical standards.

Book Design by HmdPublishing.com

Printed in the United States of America

DEDICATION

First and foremost, I have to give a special thank you to my Lord and Savior, Jesus Christ, for blessing me with the vision, strength, and grace to write these words. I don't know where I would be without your mercy and the constant reminders that healing is holy. Every revelation, every pause, every breakthrough—I give it all back to You.

To my mother, your love, sacrifice, and desire to give me more than what you were given have shaped me more than you will ever know. Thank you for having the courage to want to parent from a different place, even when it wasn't easy. You planted seeds that are now bearing fruit.

To my husband, thank you for partnering with me to embark on this wild but sweet journey of parenting with intention. I love the legacy we are leaving for our girls, and I couldn't imagine doing this with anyone else. Your steady love is the ground I stand on.

To my babies—my three daughters—Mommy can't wait to see what you offer to the world. You are already leaving your mark in the most beautiful, light-filled ways. I wrote this for us. You inspire everything.

And finally, to the cycle-breakers, the generational healers, the mothers with an innate sense of vowing to do it differently even when they don't have a roadmap—this book is for you. Thank you for your unwavering faith, relentless hope, and willingness to do the hard work of healing in real time. Your courage echoes into the future.

CONTENTS

Introduction 5

REFLECT

01| This Stops With Me 12
02| The Ghosts In The Room.. 18
03| Who You Had To Be 28
04| Listening To The Woman Inside The Mom.. 36

INTERRUPT

05| Your Body Knows The Pattern.. 47
06| Under The Guilt Is Just A Wound 55
07| Finding Stillness In The Storm 66

SHIFT

08| You Don't Have To Overgive To Be A Good Mom .. .. .. .77
09| Love Doesn't Always Sound Like Yes. 84
10| They Learn To Feel From You 91

EMBODY

11| The Story They'll Remember Starts Here.. 101
12| This Is What Coming Home Feels Like 108

Conclusion 118
Next Steps. 121
About The Author.. 124

INTRODUCTION

I remember the exact moment when I knew something had to change. I was standing in my kitchen, exhausted, overwhelmed, overstimulated, and one breath away from tears. My kids were bickering, the house was a mess, and I felt that all-too-familiar frustration rising in my chest. And then it happened—I heard my own voice, sharp and frustrated, snapping at them in a way that sounded just like my mother when she was at her wits' end.

It stopped me in my tracks.

Now, don't get it twisted—my mother is everything. She is the mom all the kids wished could be theirs. She has the biggest heart, will give her last without hesitation, and loves with a sweetness that makes everyone feel safe and cared for. She is warm, nurturing, and selfless. But she also struggled. She gave so much that there was nothing left for herself. Tapping into self-care, emotional care—those things weren't modeled for her, and as much as she poured into us, I saw the toll it took.

She wanted to be patient. She wanted to be calm. But she was carrying so much—managing a home, raising three kids, handling life's pressures, and battling her own health concerns. And when it all became too much, she would snap, yell, or shut down. Not because she was mean or unloving, but because she was depleted.

And now, here I was—doing the same thing.

The realization hit me hard. I wasn't just reacting in the moment but replaying a script I had inherited. And if I didn't make a change, my children would one day do the same. I didn't want to pass this down. I wanted a different story for my family. I wanted to parent from a place of intention, with grace, and deep connection, not out of frustration, stress, or old patterns I never consciously chose.

Right there in the middle of the kitchen chaos, I did something radical. I paused. I took a deep breath—shaky, but intentional. I dropped down to my knees, eye level with my kids, and said, "I'm sorry. I'm not proud of the way I just spoke to you. I'm overwhelmed, and that's not your fault. Can we start over?"

They looked surprised, then softened. We all did. That moment cracked something open in me.

After they went to bed that evening, I opened a journal and poured everything out. Not just the day's events, but the years of pain, pressure, exhaustion, guilt, and the old wounds I hadn't realized I was carrying and had absorbed without question. I didn't have a roadmap yet, but I had made a vow: *This cycle ends with me.*

From that day on, I started small—because that's all I could manage. I began by paying attention to my triggers, noticing the moments I felt tension rising and asking myself, *"What do I really need right now?"* I gave myself permission to slow down. I set reminders to take deep breaths. I stopped expecting perfection and started practicing presence. I created little pockets of calm—sometimes that just meant closing the bathroom door for two minutes to regroup or stepping outside to get my heart rate down and reminding myself that I'm not a bad mom, just a human having a hard moment.

I began swapping late-night scrolling for short parenting videos and journaled through old wounds during nap time. I didn't overhaul my life overnight. I simply made one intentional choice at a time: to speak with more curiosity, to apologize without shame, to pause instead of react.

And over time, those small, daily shifts added up. I wasn't just reacting less—I was connecting more. I was showing my kids what it looks like to grow, even as a grown-up.

I wasn't going to try to parent perfectly, but I *was* going to parent intentionally. I was going to slow down, get curious, and learn to lead with connection instead of control. We still have hard days, but now we have tools. We have language. We have grace.

And that's exactly why this book exists.

That moment in the kitchen didn't just change how I parent. It changed how I live. This book was born from that kitchen-floor moment—and the hundreds of intentional, imperfect choices I've made since.

It's for the mom who's always "on" but rarely feels *present*.

For the woman who promised she'd do it differently, but finds herself stuck in the same old reactions.

For the one who feels like she's failing, even though she's giving it everything she has.

I see you. I *was* you. And at times, I am still you. I want you to know—your story can shift too.

If you've ever thought…

"Why am I yelling when I don't want to?"

"I love my kids—so why do I feel so disconnected?"

"I don't want to pass this down…But I don't know how to change it…"

…then this book is for you.

But I'll be real—this isn't a quick fix or a tidy list of parenting hacks. This book is for the *cycle-breakers*. The deep feelers. The moms who are done white-knuckling their way through motherhood and are ready to gently unlearn the patterns they inherited.

This is for the women who want to lead with *presence* instead of pressure.

Grace instead of guilt. *Connection* instead of control.

What You'll Learn Inside

Through stories, simple frameworks, and reflection prompts, this book will walk you through the same foundational steps that helped me—and now help the women I work with—move from survival mode to conscious, connected parenting.

You'll learn how to:

- Understand your reactions instead of shaming them
- Break the generational patterns you didn't choose, but *can* end
- Regulate your emotions in real time
- Set boundaries without guilt
- Apologize without shame and model true repair
- Parents with clarity, confidence, and compassion

You'll also walk through the R.I.S.E. Method, my healing framework that moves you from reactive to regulated, from inherited scripts to intentional, heart-centered leadership in your home.

Now it wouldn't sit right with me if I didn't acknowledge a few mistakes I made along the way (*so you don't have to*).

I tried to just "try harder."

No amount of trying harder could carry the weight of motherhood's emotions. I needed grace, support, and God to meet me right where I was.

I felt like I had to "get it right" all the time.

I thought if I learned enough, I'd become some calm, zen mom who never raised her voice. Spoiler: I'm not. But I *am* learning to pause, apologize, and try again without the shame spiral.

I neglected my own needs.

I focused so much on parenting better that I forgot to care for myself. Turns out, you can't give what you never pause to refill.

I tried to change everything at once.

What actually created lasting transformation? *Small, steady, compassionate shifts.*

This Is the Moment Everything Changes

You don't need to become someone else to be a good mom. You just need to become more *you*. More aligned. More aware. More present.

That's what this book will help you do.

So, take a deep breath. You're not broken. You're not behind. You're just beginning.

And this time? **You get to write the story differently.**

Welcome home.

PART ONE
REFLECT

Before we can change the story, we must understand how it was written.

In this first part of the journey, we don't rush into fixing. We don't bypass the pain or leap into solutions. We slow down. We look inward. We get honest.

Because the patterns we want to shift didn't start with us, and they don't define us either. They were passed down in silence, shame, survival, and sacrifice. Reflecting is how we break the cycle of rinse, cycle, and repeat. It's how we start to see the invisible scripts we've been carrying, and begin to ask: *"Do I want to keep passing this on?"*

In these chapters, we will explore the emotional inheritance you've received (Chapter 2), the roles you learned to play to stay safe (Chapter 3), and the truth of the woman inside the mom (Chapter 4). But first, we begin where all change begins—with a bold, brave declaration:

This stops with me.

You are not just parenting your child. You're reparenting yourself. These next chapters will help you make sense of your reactions, your guilt, your tenderness, and your truth. We don't do this with shame. We do it with curiosity. With compassion. With courage.

Let's begin.

01 | THIS STOPS WITH ME

"Perhaps you were born for such a time as this."
— **Esther 4:14 (NIV)**

Store personnel reported to the aisle to clean up the scattered Fruit Loops and Cheerios that decorated the floor.

Reflecting back on that moment, I remember the look of defeat and embarrassment on her face as onlookers gawked and shook their heads in disapproval.

Just a moment of overwhelm got the best of her, and she was reaching for anything—authority, volume, a sense of order—to get through the spiraling chaos of the moment.

But as a child, I couldn't help but think, does it really take all of that to get a child to listen?

This was one of the many thoughts that paid my mind a visit that day while out grocery shopping with my daddy and witnessing a mother tear into her child over knocking down some cereal boxes.

Fast forward to now, and I can casually say, *"I get it."* She was not a bad mother—she was a worn-out one, and I can see now that her outburst was a cry for help, not a permanent indictment of her parenting.

That mother was trying to survive what should have been a normal day at the grocery store, but now she was faced with public shame, inner guilt, and the impossible pressure of being seen but not falling apart.

And the child? Completely frozen—eyes wide, lips quivering, and scared of what would come.

To be honest, no one wants to be "that parent," the one who loses it in aisle five, but when you feel as if your back is against the wall, you default to what gives the illusion of safety and control.

You reach for what's familiar, what's known for getting a parent through the trenches, when in fact, it was the very thing that once wounded the child you used to be. And now, I wonder what impact that had on the child? I could only imagine what the blow-up would look like if that child made a "big" mistake.

A part of me had the urge to step in—to make everything okay, to help the mama so she didn't have to carry the weight of her unraveling alone, even if just for a moment.

And the other part of me wanted to say to the child, "It's okay to mess up. Grown-ups do it too. You're just trying your best in a world that sometimes forgets how little you still are."

In fact, if I could go back in time and give that mother a chance at a re-do, I'd wrap her in grace, not judgment, and whisper, "You get to choose differently now. The cycle can end here. It doesn't have to be this way anymore." *This stops with you.*

This is where your journey inward begins. Not into your child. Not into another parenting technique or strategy. But into *you*.

Right now, we aren't trying to fix anything. We are simply holding up a mirror and gently mapping the emotional terrain of what shaped you. Because the way you mother today didn't start with you. It started generations back, with what was passed down, what was normalized, and what was never allowed to be felt.

And now, you are the woman brave enough to pause, look, and say: *"This cycle ends with me."*

And like the mother, I welcome you, mama, to safely land in a space that allows you to let go of the guilt you've been carrying, entertain the possibility of doing things differently without shame, and rest in knowing that breaking the cycle doesn't require you to have it all figured out, only to be willing.

With that said, let's begin this chapter not with a lecture, but with a moment. Maybe it will sound familiar.

You're walking inside the front door of your home. The house is loud. The mess is multiplying. Your kids are arguing, and something small—spilled milk, a sharp tone, a toy thrown across the room—pushes you past your edge. You snap. Loud. Sharp. Too much.

Instantly, there's silence.

But inside, a storm rages. Shame. Guilt. Loneliness---the kind that whispers, *"No one really sees how hard I'm trying."*

You retreat. Maybe to the bathroom. Maybe to the bedroom. Maybe just into your own thoughts. And you whisper, *"I don't want to be this kind of mom."*

If this stirs something in you, know this: you're not carrying it alone.

That moment? That's your *invitation*. It might feel like rock bottom, but it's also a doorway. A sacred one. The first moment of clarity that says: *This isn't working. And I'm ready to begin again.*

We don't parent in a vacuum. We parent from memory, muscle, and maps handed to us long before we had our own kids.

For many of us, those maps were marked by love, yes—but also by silence, survival, and systems prioritizing obedience over connection. We learned what love looked like through discipline, what safety felt like through control, and how to suppress emotion just to keep the peace.

And so, when the pressure rises, our body doesn't reach for logic. It reaches for the familiar.

I remember the moment I realized I was sounding just like my mother in her most overwhelmed moments. Not because she was cold or distant, but because she had spent years holding everyone else up, and no one taught her how to hold herself. Her voice became mine. Her patterns lived in me.

That realization wasn't about blame. It was about clarity. I wasn't failing. I was *replaying*. Replaying unspoken rules, inherited fears, and survival strategies that didn't start with me, but were living through me.

And that's why this first step is called **The Mirror.**

It's about pausing to reflect on what you were shown, what you absorbed, and what parts of you were shaped before you ever had a say.

Take a moment to consider:

- How did your caregivers express love? Anger? Stress? Affection?
- What was the emotional tone of your home growing up?
- What kinds of behavior were praised? What was punished?
- What did "being a good child" mean in your family?

These reflections aren't here to shame your past—they're here to help you understand your present.

Here's the truth: Awareness doesn't fix everything. But it changes everything.

The moment you recognize that your reactions aren't coming out of nowhere—that they are rooted in patterns you didn't choose—you unlock something powerful: *choice.*

And here's the concept I want to teach you in this chapter:

Your reactions are rooted in your emotional blueprint, but you are allowed to redraw the lines.

When you feel triggered, frustrated, or overwhelmed, it's not always about the moment in front of you. Often, it's about something much older. A belief you inherited. A tone you internalized. A pattern your body memorized to stay safe.

Try asking yourself:

- What parts of my parenting feel instinctive, but are actually inherited?
- What do I fear will happen if I parent differently than I was raised?
- What's one pattern I want to understand, not just stop?

It's not easy to look at the parts of us we were never allowed to name. It takes courage to say, "I don't want to pass this down. But I don't know how to do it differently."

And that's okay. This chapter isn't about having all the answers. It's about being willing to ask better questions.

Let me be clear: Reactivity does *not* make you a bad mom.

It makes you human. It makes you someone who's likely under-supported, over-stretched, and running patterns that were never yours to begin with.

When you snap, it doesn't mean you're broken. It means something inside you is begging to be seen, soothed, and supported.

You're not bad. You're patterned.

And patterns can be rewritten.

One mom I worked with shared how bedtime always ended in tension. She'd try to stay patient, but the resistance from her child triggered something deep in her. One night, after snapping and seeing the fear in her daughter's eyes, she realized, *"That's what I used to feel growing up."*

She didn't need a script. She needed support.

And she began—not by getting it perfect, but by getting curious. That moment became her mirror.

The fact that you're reading this means you've already started. This is the moment where something old begins to loosen, and something new begins to grow.

You don't need to be perfect to break the cycle. You don't need to have it all figured out. You just need to be willing to pause. To notice. To reflect.

The cycle stops not because you never mess up again. It stops because *when* you do, you choose to repair. You choose to return. You choose a different way forward.

And that? That is sacred work.

Reflection Prompt:

What do I want to end with me, and what do I want to begin with me?

Next, we'll explore how to gently trace your emotional blueprint—what was modeled, what was missing, and what you're ready to redefine. But for now, take a breath.

You saw something clearly today. And that changes everything.

02 | THE GHOSTS IN THE ROOM

"Sometimes the loudest voices in the room are the ones no one else can hear."
- **Author Unknown**

He wasn't upset about the iPad anymore. He was scared of *her*.

The room was silent, but it didn't feel empty. She stood in her living room, hands clenched by her sides, staring down at her six-year-old who had just shattered the family iPad. He stared back—wide-eyed, lip trembling, a mix of fear and confusion hidden behind his tears.

She wanted to say something calm, kneel and cradle him, and ask if he was okay. But instead, her voice came out sharp, louder than she intended. "What is wrong with you?! Do you ever think before you act??"

The words hit the air like the truth no one wanted to name. They weren't new—not to her.

In that moment, she wasn't just a mother. She was a daughter again—seven years old, back in her childhood kitchen, flinching under her father's booming voice.

"Why do you always mess things up?"

What stung more was how he looked at her—like she was a problem to fix, not a child who'd made a mistake. Her hands had shaken as she swept up the broken pieces from the coffee mug she dropped. She'd barely spoken the rest of the night. Neither had he nor her mother, ever looked up from the dishes.

She remembered standing in the hallway afterward, heart pounding, whispering a promise to herself: *When I have kids, I'll never make them feel like this.*

But what exactly *was* "this"?

She hadn't known how to name it at the time—she was only seven—but now, as an adult, she could finally put words to it.

Unworthy. Alone. Like a disappointment. Like her mistakes made her unlovable. Like her presence was too much—and not enough—at the same time.

She remembered how she'd stared at the floorboards, too scared to cry, because crying made things worse. Her body had gone still, locked tight. Even at that age, she had already learned the unspoken rule: *Don't feel too much. Don't ask for comfort. Fix it, clean it, and don't make a scene.*

That was the night she learned to handle everything by herself. The night she told herself: *If I just try harder, they'll stop being mad.*

That was the real cost of those old reactions. Not just the yelling or the fear, but the quiet belief it planted in a child: *That mistakes make you unworthy. That connection can disappear in a flash.* And that feeling? She prayed that her kids would never have to carry it.

So, how *did* she want them to feel? Safe, loved, even when they mess up, and valued for who they are, not just what they do right.

She wanted her kids to know that they didn't have to be perfect to be accepted. That emotions weren't dangerous. That home was a place where they could fall apart and still be held close.

And most of all, she wanted them to know that their worst moment wouldn't erase her love.

And yet here she was. Her son stood in front of her, frozen in the same posture she had once known. Shoulders curled in. Chest held tight. Tears welled but were not yet free. He was overcome by the weight of emotion his body carried—but he wasn't shutting down to defy her—he was *afraid*.

He wasn't scared of the broken tablet. He was scared of *her*.

That realization landed with brutal clarity.

She sank to the couch, burying her face in her hands. She wasn't angry anymore—just gutted. Her son hadn't just cracked a screen. He'd cracked open something buried: an old wound, still raw underneath after all those years.

She looked up at him, blinking back her own tears.

"Come here," she whispered.

He didn't move at first. She softened her voice. "I'm not mad anymore. I want to talk."

He stepped toward her cautiously, and she pulled him gently into her arms. He resisted for a moment, unsure, but then melted into her chest.

"I'm sorry, I scared you". "That wasn't about you. That was... me remembering something I've tried hard to forget."

He didn't understand her words fully, but he understood the warmth returning to her voice. The safety. The shift.

She sat there with him, holding him close, thinking about how easy it is to carry the past into the present. And how hard it is to stop it.

And that's when it hit her—none of us parents alone.

Even if your partner is at work, even if you're the only adult in the house, even if the baby's asleep or your toddler's lost in a snack-fueled YouTube binge—there are still others in the room. Not actual people. But mental guests. Echoes. Imprints. There are ghosts in the room. Not the spooky kind. The emotional kind. The ones we inherited.

You may be the only adult physically present, but emotionally? You're often parenting *with your mother's voice in your head. With your father's silence. With the rules your childhood taught you about love, control, obedience, and shame.*

These "ghosts" don't shout. They whisper. They show up in the tension in your chest, the need for control in the chaos, the phrase that slips out before you realize you've said it—*"Because I said so!"*

This chapter isn't about judging those ghosts. It's about finally *seeing them.*

Because you can't interrupt what you haven't noticed.

And the moment you begin to see what's influencing you... is the moment you begin to break free.

You were holding it together—barely.

Your child slams a door.

It's loud. Abrupt. But manageable.

You were tired.

But you were trying. You were doing the "gentle voice". The redirection. The breathing that felt more like survival than relief.

Yet something inside you *flares.* Your whole body tenses. Your jaw tightens. You raise your voice—maybe sharper than you'd like. And as the dust settles, you ask yourself: *Why did that moment feel so much bigger than it was?*

Because that moment wasn't just about your child.

It was about *you.* The child you once were. The tone you grew up around. The rules you were taught. Maybe it was the memory of being told not to "talk back," being punished for having big feelings, or the unspoken fear that anger wasn't safe.

These aren't just memories. They're imprints. Ghosts.

And then—someone screamed. The juice spilled. Your youngest hit your oldest. Someone told you they "hate this house."

And before you could stop it, *you were giving them a piece of your mind.*

It wasn't just a raised voice. It was the kind of yell that slips out when everything inside feels too heavy to hold. The kind that startles even you. That fills the room with tension and leaves your children still watching, wondering what just happened. It's not until the words leave your mouth that you realize: *You've said this before.* Or rather, *someone else said it to you.*

And now, here you are, re-enacting the very scene that played on a loop in your childhood home.

And it guts you because this is *not* the mother you want to be. You love your kids. Deeply. Fiercely. But in that moment, it didn't feel like love leading.

Who you're trying so hard to be—the calm, gentle, present mom—is fighting a quiet battle with the way you were wired to survive growing up.

Maybe it was your mother. Your father. A caregiver from your childhood.

Maybe it wasn't what they said, but how it made you feel: silenced, small, unseen.

Now here you are, saying it. Not because you want to—but because it's *in you.* Rehearsed. Replayed. Remembered.

This isn't a setback or you getting it wrong. It's your body's way of showing you where healing still wants to happen.

You're here now. And this chapter is about learning how to take the reins back.

Because you can love your children, and still be carrying pain you didn't ask for. But the cycle ends *when you see it.* When you say, "Not this time. Not like this."

Ghosts aren't people. They're patterns. Messages. Rules. Emotional energy passed down from generation to generation.

They are the unspoken beliefs we absorbed, even if no one ever said them out loud:

- "Crying is weak."
- "Don't air our dirty laundry."

- "Obedience equals love."
- "You're only lovable when you're quiet, helpful, or good."

And these beliefs don't just live in your mind. They live in your *body*. In your nervous system. In the way your heart races when your child cries. In the urgency to fix their emotions, or shut them down.

These ghosts come in different forms:

- **The Enforcer:** "This is just how it's always been."
- **The Silencer:** "We don't talk about that."
- **The Protector:** "We did the best we could."

Each of these ghosts had a purpose in the past. Some protected us. Some taught us how to survive. But if we don't name them, they continue to lead our parenting, often without our consent.

These ghosts don't always show up harshly. Sometimes, they wear the costume of "wisdom" or "what good mothers do." But if you listen closely, you'll hear the cost.

- Tired? *"You can rest once the kids are in bed."*
  → Message: *Your needs come last. Always.*
  → Internal voice: *So what if I'm about to break?*
- Stressed? *"This is just what parenting is—it's hard."*
  → Message: *Exhaustion is a badge of honor.*
  → Internal voice: *So I should just suck it up?*
- Overwhelmed? *"Kids should appreciate how hard we work for them."*
  → Message: *Your worth is tied to your productivity.*
  → Internal voice: *So if they struggle, they're ungrateful?*
- Emotional? *"You don't fall apart. You just get things done."*
  → Message: *Feelings are inconvenient.*
  → Internal voice: *If I slow down, I'll fail.*

These aren't just bad habits. They're survival strategies passed down by people doing the best they could.

And if you don't stop and *see them*, they'll keep leading.

Let's name this, too:

Not everything we inherit is a ghost. Some of it is gold.

There are patterns worth keeping.

Maybe your mom showed up for every school event, even if she was tired.

Maybe your dad tucked you in with a story every night, no matter how old you got. Maybe your family made birthdays sacred, held each other through grief, or taught you the power of laughter in hard moments.

You're allowed to keep what still serves you. You're allowed to bless it, expand it, and pass it on with pride.

This isn't about clearing the slate. It's about consciously choosing what becomes part of *your family's story*.

You are the filter. You are the voice that gets to say: *This stays. That ends here.*

And as you parent your child, you're not doing it in a vacuum. You're in conversation with your child, with your past, and the version of you that's still unfolding.

Three voices shape every moment with your child:

1. **The child in front of you**
2. **The child you once were**
3. **The parent you're trying to become**

The challenge? The first two often speak first.

Your current child triggers something in your past child, and suddenly, your nervous system reacts before your wiser self has a chance to speak.

This doesn't mean you're broken. It means your past is louder than your present, *for now*.

But that can change. And awareness is where it starts. You don't need a perfect plan to break a pattern. You just need a moment. A breath. A pause.

Here's a tool to help you separate your true voice from the ghosts that show up in your parenting.

The Pattern Interrupt Practice:
1. **Pause:** Notice the reaction rising in your body.
2. **Name It:** Ask yourself, *"This feels familiar... Is this mine?"*
3. **Breathe:** Create just a sliver of space between feeling and action.
4. **Choose Differently:** Ask, *"What does this moment actually need?"*

Let's break that down with a real example.

Without the pattern interrupt:

"Why can't you ever just listen!?"

With the pattern interrupt:

Pause. Breathe. "I'm getting really overwhelmed right now. I need a minute, and then we'll talk."

That single breath? That pause? It's not small. It's *revolutionary*.

One mom told me she didn't recognize herself when her daughter cried.

Something about it triggered her deeply. She wasn't trying to be harsh, but she'd hear herself say things like, "You're fine. That's enough."

Afterward, she'd feel gutted.

Through our work, she remembered how unsafe it felt to cry as a kid. Her father didn't yell but dismissed her ability to safely feel. The message was clear: strong girls don't break down.

She wasn't trying to pass that down. But it was there.

The ghost was alive in her tone, her tension, her instinct to shut it down.

We practiced the Pattern Interrupt together. The next time her daughter cried, she paused. Breathed. And said, "It's okay to cry. I'm here."

Her daughter softened.

Not because she changed, but because *her mother did.*

Let's begin this sacred noticing together.

Try keeping a "Ghost Log" this week. Nothing fancy—just a note in your phone or a small journal entry when you sense a reaction that feels... *not yours.*

Use these prompts to help:

- When I said _____, it sounded like _____.
- When I felt triggered by _____, it reminded me of _____.
- What was never allowed in my home growing up?
- What unspoken rule am I still following?

This isn't about blame.

This is about *liberation.*

Just because a voice shows up... doesn't mean it has to lead.

Key Takeaway

Your reactions are not random. They're rehearsed. Written long ago by people who were doing the best they could, but who passed down survival, not sovereignty.

You are allowed to choose a new story. You are allowed to parent from presence, not programming. You are allowed to honor your past without repeating it.

The ghost may whisper.

But you get to speak last.

Reflection Prompt

As you start to listen to within, I want you to practice noticing, without judgment, what voices live in you. Ask yourself:

What voices have I inherited—and which ones do I want to stop echoing forward? Which ones feel true, and which were just survival?

This is how you begin to choose with intention, not just replay old patterns.

03 | WHO YOU HAD TO BE

> *"An identity would seem to be arrived at by the way in which the person faces and uses his experience."*
> — **James Baldwin**

It started with a Pinterest board and ended with a panic attack in the bathroom.

She had spent three weeks planning her son's preschool Valentine's party. Handmade treat bags. A sensory station. Allergy-friendly snacks. Heart-shaped fruit kabobs. The other moms had just signed up to bring juice or napkins, but her? She built an entire theme around *"Love is Learning."* She even made laminated name tags.

For her, going the extra mile meant showing up in ways that couldn't be ignored—making things "perfect" so no one could question her value. She didn't just meet expectations. She worked herself to the edge to exceed them, every time. It was how she had learned to feel worthy: by being exceptional.

She told herself it was because she loved doing it and that it was for her son. That she *wanted* to go the extra mile.

But the truth came out in the preschool hallway, two minutes before the party started, when another mom casually walked in with store-bought cupcakes and said, "I wish I had time to do all this stuff like you do."

She smiled. But inside? Her chest tightened. Her stomach flipped. That one sentence somehow confirmed the fear she never said out loud:

If I'm not doing the most, will anyone even see me?

She excused herself to the bathroom, locked the door, and sat on the closed toilet lid, trembling. She didn't know if she was anxious, angry, or just tired—maybe all three.

That's when it hit her.

This wasn't really about the Valentine's party.

It was about who she had to be growing up.

The overachiever. The high performer. The one who got straight A's, racked up awards, made the honor roll, and stayed busy enough to outrun the loneliness in her house. The one who felt as if she wasn't succeeding at something, she might disappear altogether.

She didn't grow up with chaos. She grew up with a quiet distance. Her parents weren't unkind, just emotionally unavailable. They noticed her report cards more than her tears. So she learned: achievement got attention. Feelings didn't.

And now here she was, decades later, still trying to earn her place—this time through glittery crafts and themed snack trays.

She thought about her son. Earlier that morning, he'd tugged on her sleeve as she assembled the treat bags. "Mom, can you play Legos with me now?" She had looked at the clock, then the half-assembled decorations, and said, "In a little bit, okay? I have to finish this first."

He had nodded and walked away quietly. She hadn't thought much of it at the time.

But now, sitting in that tiny bathroom, it hit her: She had said no to connection so she could chase perfection.

That was the cost. Not just her energy, but moments with the person she was doing it all *for*.

She didn't feel proud. She felt grief.

Grief for how hard she had always tried. For how invisible she felt unless she was over-performing. And now, for how easily she had passed that pressure onto a four-year-old who just wanted to play.

What if I don't need to prove anything anymore?

She wiped her face, stood up, and looked at herself in the mirror. She didn't look like someone failing. She looked like someone finally getting honest.

It is a pivotal moment in every mother's life when she realizes she's not just parenting her child but also herself. The child who once had to be perfect, quiet, agreeable, or strong is still in her, clinging to survival mechanisms built long ago.

They've carried her through life, kept her safe when love was conditional, or fear was overwhelming. But now, as she steps into motherhood, those protective parts of herself are no longer just helpers. They're loud, unresolved parts of you—and they demand attention.

Because for the first time, your body is asking you to notice what it never had the space to process.

You are not alone in this. You carry not only your current self, but also the child you once were—the one who learned how to survive in a chaotic or uncertain environment. Somewhere in your childhood home, you learned what was expected of you. But at what cost?

Maybe no one ever said it out loud, but you got the message: "This is what it takes to stay safe. This is who you have to be to feel love, to avoid punishment, to stay connected." These expectations shaped your self-worth, emotional life, and ability to navigate the world. They were survival tools at the time, but they've followed you into your adult life, now showing up in ways you might not even recognize.

Perhaps it meant being helpful. Quiet. Smart. Put-together. Maybe it was about staying small, saying sorry before you'd even done anything, or never letting your emotions take up too much space.

Maybe it meant being the peacekeeper, the one who didn't make waves, who soothed others' emotions before tending to your own.

Or maybe it meant learning to be the strong one, the resilient one who didn't ask for help, the one who held everything together. It could have meant being the "fixer"—the one who fixed broken hearts, systems, or situations—or simply the one who did what was needed to keep things moving.

And that version of you? She's still here. Still trying. Still working hard to protect you, especially in motherhood, where so much of what we never processed comes rushing to the surface.

You might not even realize it's happening. You just know that you freeze when your child cries. Or you spiral when someone's upset with you. Or you feel a deep pull to fix everything, even when you're already at capacity.

You wonder, "Why am I like this? Why do I feel like I can't stop?"

Here's the answer that changed everything for me:

You're not broken or damaged.

You're just still acting from a role that once kept you safe.

And when you start seeing that role clearly, not judging it, not shaming it, just *seeing* it, you begin to realize: who you had to be back then… doesn't have to lead now.

I remember one of those moments. It was late. I was exhausted. I had done the snacks, the stories, the bath, the teeth, the full bedtime song and dance. And still, my child was crying. Wanting more of me. More time. More soothing. I could feel my body tightening. My thoughts getting loud. My breath caught in my chest.

And without thinking, I blurted, "You're fine. You don't need anything else. You need to go to sleep."

Instant regret. Shame, even. She wasn't being difficult; she was just yearning for more connection after a new start at school. New change, new people, new rhythms…and she was looking for me to help her safely rebalance her world. But I missed it in the moment. I saw resistance when it was really a reach for reassurance. And the guilt of that misunderstanding hit hard.

Later, when I journaled it out, I realized something powerful: I wasn't reacting to my child—I was reacting to an old belief that I carried like armor. The belief that my needs weren't allowed. That expressing anything too loudly would make me a burden. That being "too much" would lead to rejection.

I spent a great deal of my childhood being helpful. Easy. The one who didn't cause problems. The one who figured it out. And now here I was, a mother—and I still couldn't let someone need me without it feeling like a threat.

That's when I began to really understand the difference between who I am… and who I had to be.

We all carry these roles. They were our survival strategies. Our emotional protectors.

Some of us learned to be "The Good Girl." We knew we'd be safer if we stayed small, sweet, and agreeable. We'd be praised. We'd be less likely to provoke disappointment.

Some of us became "The Overachiever." We discovered that doing more, earning more, and winning more love through performance made us feel worthy, even if we were silently falling apart.

Some became "The Peacemaker." We carried everyone else's emotions, tried to keep the house calm, even if it meant we were never honest about how we really felt.

Some of us had to become "The Caretaker." Maybe our parents were emotionally absent or overwhelmed, and we learned to read the room, anticipate needs, soothe the chaos—because if we didn't, no one would.

Others became "The Invisible One." We learned to stay quiet, unnoticed. We minimized our presence so we wouldn't be seen as a problem.

And some of us became "The Rebel." We fought to be heard. We used our voice to protect our tenderness. We pushed back because vulnerability felt unsafe.

The thing is, these roles *worked*. They protected us. They made sense at the time.

But now, as mothers, they often reappear in moments we least expect. And the cost? Disconnection. Guilt. Exhaustion. Frustration. Low sense of self-worth. All at the expense of feeling like we're performing instead of parenting.

A client once told me she couldn't understand why her daughter's big emotions made her so angry. She would literally lose it. Not because she wanted to—but because something in her body went rigid, like her daughter's sadness was a threat.

When we explored her story, she realized she grew up with the message that crying was weak. That sadness made you dramatic. That keeping it together was the only way to be lovable.

So, she learned to be strong. Composed. Emotionally controlled. And now, her daughter's vulnerability was poking the very wound she had spent a lifetime avoiding.

That's the truth about these roles: they're not flaws. They're reflections of what you had to do to survive your environment. But the role that protected you in childhood may now prevent you from connecting in parenting, partnership, and with yourself.

This is why I take great care in teaching the concept of *Protective Roles vs. Present Selves.*

Protective roles are the masks we wear to avoid rejection, shame, or pain. They're rehearsed. Automatic. They whisper, "This is what keeps you safe." The key here is that these roles were created for survival. They kept you safe when you were younger. But they were based on the assumption that you weren't allowed to need, feel, or express certain things.

But your present self, the mother you're becoming, is wise. Curious. Capable of choosing something new. And every time you pause to notice a reaction, to question an old script, to choose a softer tone or a slower pace, you're stepping into that present self.

In this moment, with your child, you have the power to choose a new story. One that is grounded in the mother you want to be, not the child you were.

You don't have to drop your role overnight. You just have to notice when it shows up.

That noticing is the invitation.

It sounds like, "Wow... I just apologized again for having a boundary. That's my 'Good Girl' talking." Or, "I stayed up late doing everything myself instead of asking for help. That's my 'Caretaker' still running the show."

That's not weakness. That's awareness. And awareness is the first breath of change.

If you want a place to begin, try this: the next time you feel that tight, automatic pull to fix, please, prove, or disappear—pause. Place a hand on your chest. And whisper to yourself:

"I don't have to be who I had to be. What would my present self do in this moment?"

You get to respond from the woman you are now, not the girl who had to stay small.

Maybe today, that looks like letting yourself cry. Maybe it's letting the laundry wait. Maybe it's saying no without a follow-up paragraph. Maybe it's letting your child be upset without fixing it.

Each moment you do that, you're interrupting the role and you start to give yourself the grace to act in ways that reflect who you are *now*.

Because who you are underneath the performance is someone your child needs to see. Someone *you* deserve to be.

You're allowed to be seen without the script. Loved without the mask.

Free from the roles that once protected you, but no longer serve you.

And that is how the cycle begins to shift.

Reflection Prompt:

So now, as you sit with all of this—not in shame, but in curiosity—ask yourself gently:

What roles did I learn to play as a child… and where are they still leading the show?

Where do they whisper old messages into my modern motherhood?

And who might I be—what kind of mother, woman, human—if I no longer needed to perform, prove, or protect to feel worthy?

Take a breath here. You're not rewriting your past. You're reclaiming your presence.

Let these questions be a soft beginning. The kind that doesn't demand an answer right away—but makes space for something new to unfold.

04 | LISTENING TO THE WOMAN INSIDE THE MOM

> *"There's a voice beneath the noise of motherhood—it's yours. And she doesn't need fixing. She needs honoring."*
> **-Unknown**

Everyone had an opinion, but none of them were in the room at 2 a.m.

The baby was crying again. 2:08 a.m., and this mom was on night four of broken sleep, pacing the living room with her daughter on her shoulder, her back aching, her mind buzzing.

She had tried *everything*.

Swaddle tighter. Swaddle looser. White noise. No noise. Bottle. No bottle.

She'd googled reflux, colic, and baby gas at least a dozen times. Scrolled forums. Saved Instagram posts. Read three blogs that contradicted each other. Called her mom. Texted her sister.

Everyone had a different opinion, and none of them was working.

Standing there in the blue glow of the baby monitor, she felt a wave of shame rise in her chest. *Why don't I know what I'm doing?*

And then another thought, quieter but clearer: *Or... maybe I do. Maybe I just haven't learned to trust it yet.*

That voice was so subtle, it almost got drowned out by the noise of "shoulds."

You should let her cry.

You should feed her again.

You should sleep-train.

You should co-sleep.

You should toughen up.

You should stop holding her so much.

You should know better by now.

She had spent most of her life doing what she was told.

She learned early on that following directions earned approval, staying quiet kept the peace, and questioning things only led to tension. So she made herself small to avoid conflict and shaped herself around other people's needs. Over time, she became the kind of person who didn't just follow the rules—she *relied* on them, because they gave her a sense of security in a world where emotional safety often felt out of reach.

She had been the responsible one. The agreeable one. The "easy" kid who followed the rules and didn't push back, because being liked felt safer than being herself. She became the adult who second-guessed everything, even when her gut was screaming at her. Who confused being "good" with being obedient. Who had learned to ignore her own knowing, just to stay out of trouble.

So, of course, she was struggling now. Because *motherhood doesn't come with a script, and she had been trained her whole life to follow one.*

That night, something shifted. It wasn't dramatic or loud. It was quiet. Small. She stopped pacing. Sat down on the couch. Pulled her daughter to her chest.

She didn't try another trick. Didn't scroll for answers. She just held her.

"I've got you," she whispered. "Even if I don't have it all figured out yet."

Her daughter kept crying for a few more minutes, but then, slowly, softened, and so did this mama.

It wasn't the end of the struggle, not by a long shot. But it was the beginning of something different: Listening to herself. Trusting her instincts and believing that the wisdom she needed wasn't in a headline or a hot take—it was *already inside her*.

And maybe, just maybe, she didn't have to be the girl who always followed the rules anymore.

That moment wasn't just about a crying baby or a tired mother—it was a window into something deeper. For many of us, the struggle to trust ourselves didn't start in motherhood. It started in childhood.

We learned early how to read the room. How to adapt. How to be what was needed—whether that was helpful, quiet, high-achieving, obedient, or invisible. We shaped ourselves around other people's comfort, approval, and expectations... until one day, we couldn't tell where their voices ended and our truth began.

That's what this chapter is here to gently name: the scripts you took on not because they were you, but because they protected you. This is about meeting those past versions of yourself with tenderness, not blame, and beginning the slow, brave work of coming back home to the woman underneath all the performance. The one who was there before the pleasing. Before the striving. Before the silence.

The one who still *knows*.

Not the voice of perfection. Not the voice of people-pleasing. Not the voice of all the parenting gurus who sound so confident on podcasts but haven't lived a day in your body.

It's the voice of *truth*.

This is such a pivotal shift in your journey—not because you're becoming a "better" mom, but because you're beginning to remember there's a *woman* inside the motherhood. A woman who still feels, still dreams, still matters.

You may have spent years quieting her, overriding her with advice, pressure, comparison, and the "shoulds" that seem to come with every stage of motherhood. But she's still there. Still whispering underneath the noise.

This chapter is about tuning back in.

Because beneath the roles you hold and the responsibilities you carry, there is a woman who already knows how to lead with wisdom, warmth, and inner authority. She doesn't need to yell to be heard. She just needs space.

Let's clear it for her. She's been waiting.

Maybe you've felt this too:

You finally get a quiet moment to yourself, and instead of feeling relief, you feel...lost. Not rested. Not refreshed. Just...empty. You scroll your phone. You pace the kitchen. You look at the to-do list. But underneath it all is a quiet ache that whispers, *Where did I go?*

You want to do right by your child. So, you start gathering tools. You follow respectful parenting accounts, save TikToks, listen to podcasts, and fill your bookshelf with every title from "No-Drama" to "Whole-Brain" to "Atomic Habits for Parents."

You love learning. You want to get it right.

But after a while, all that input can become noise.

Your mind loops: *Should I be firmer? Softer? Am I being too gentle? Not gentle enough? Why is this so hard for me when it seems easier for other moms?*

It's not that you don't care. It's that you're emotionally *clogged*.

Too much data. Not enough direction. The world has trained you to look outward. But the guidance you're craving? It's inward.

You haven't lost your wisdom. It just got crowded out.

Your inner knowing didn't abandon you. It's just been muffled by the noise of internalized scripts, fear of judgment, and cultural pressure to be all things to everyone.

You've been surviving—checking every box, managing every need, tending to every emotion. But the cost? Your own.

Here's how you know she's still in there:

When you pause and think, *"That didn't feel right."* When you have a quiet nudge to slow down, soften, or stay. When something inside you says, *"This moment needs presence, not performance."*

Your intuition doesn't shout. It doesn't criticize. It doesn't guilt-trip. It whispers.

"You're safe."

"Slow down."

"It's okay to rest."

But it may also speak up in other ways:

"I'm tired."

"I miss myself."

"I don't even know what I want anymore."

Sometimes the first thing your inner voice says is, *"I'm tired of being ignored."*

Because sometimes the voice of intuition isn't a wise whisper at first—it's frustration. It's tension. It's a short fuse. At the end of the day, it's a heavy sigh that says, "There has to be more to me than this."

So, let's get honest about what that voice is up against.

Not every voice that sounds familiar is actually yours. Some are transferred. Some are imposed. Some are just echoes of expectations that were never meant to define you.

Let's talk about what it looks like when old scripts are running the show versus when your inner truth is speaking.

You may have internalized messages like: "They're manipulating you." But your wiser self might sense, "They're struggling and don't know how to ask for what they need."

Or maybe the voice says, "Don't let them win." And yet deep down, something softer speaks: "This isn't a battle. It's a relationship."

There's a difference between being guided by fear and being guided by wisdom. Fear feels urgent, harsh, and rigid. Wisdom feels steady, clear, and kind.

Sometimes the voices you hear in your parenting moments might belong to the mother who never got to cry, the father who measured worth by obedience, the teacher who punished sensitivity, and the culture that told you motherhood meant self-erasure.

Try this when you feel yourself spiraling into confusion:

Ask: *What am I feeling right now?* Ask: *What do I need?* Ask: *What part of me is speaking?*

This is what I call the **Inner Inquiry**.

Is it the Fixer who thinks you're failing if you're not solving? The Critic who tells you you're not enough? Or is it the deeper, Wiser Self—the one rooted in presence and care?

Answering these three questions daily is the beginning of reconnection. It's not complicated. But it *is* powerful.

Because when you start to meet your own needs, you don't just feel better—you parent better. The mother becomes clearer, more connected, and emotionally safe when the woman is cared for.

But when the woman is silenced, the mother becomes reactive, resentful, and rigid.

You can't parent from your power if you've disconnected from your personhood.

If you've ever thought, *"I wish someone would just tell me what to do,"* I want to offer this:

Maybe that someone is *you*.

Not the you who's overwhelmed or overstimulated. Not the you who's reading six books and still second-guessing. But the *inner you* who has lived every moment of your story. The you who knows your child like no expert ever will. The you who wants peace more than perfection.

That version of you? She's not flawless. But she is present. And powerful.

You are not lost. You just haven't been given permission to trust yourself.

So here it is: You have permission.

I once worked with a mom who had tried *every* parenting method. Charts, timers, scripts, gentle corrections. And yet she kept feeling more lost, more disconnected.

One day she told me, "I finally asked myself, 'What actually feels right for me? What kind of mother do I want to be?'"

That question changed everything.

She started tuning in instead of reaching out. She stopped trying to fix every meltdown and began focusing on staying emotionally available.

And guess what? The power struggles began to ease. The connection deepened. Not because she found a perfect method. But because she found *herself*.

This is how it begins with one honest question. One exhale. One intentional choice to come back to your own wisdom.

So, let's make that choice a habit.

Every morning, before the world begins asking for your attention, take a moment to check in.

Place your hand on your heart. Close your eyes. Take three slow, intentional breaths. Ask yourself, *"What would the calm, conscious version of me need today?"* And then—listen. Whatever comes up, honor it in one small way.

You might hear: "I need a moment to myself before the chaos begins." "I need to lower my expectations." "I need to stop trying to fix everything and just sit beside them."

Your job isn't to justify that voice. Just to acknowledge it. That's how you rebuild trust.

Try this too:

- Write down the thoughts that show up in high-stress moments.
- Ask, *whose voice is this?*
- Ask, *what does my inner knowing say instead?*

Repeat until you start to feel a shift—from autopilot to awareness. From reacting to responding. From drowning in doubt to being anchored in clarity.

You might find that your own wisdom was waiting there all along. Not demanding. Just devoted.

Let these **reflection prompts** guide you deeper:

- **When was the last time I asked myself what I want?**
- **What have I stopped doing that used to bring me joy?**
- **What part of me have I silenced in the name of being "a good mom"?**

- **What might it be if I could hear one thing from my inner voice today?**

Set a three-minute timer. No pressure. Just start writing. Let it be messy. Let it be real. Let it be yours.

And when you feel unsure, remember this:

"I am still here. And I matter, too."

That quiet knowing inside you?

She's not broken. She's not gone. She's not behind.

She's simply waiting for you to come back to her.

So today, take one small step. Put your hand on your heart. Breathe. Ask her what she knows.

And then… listen.

You are the mother you've been looking for.

She's been with you all along.

PART TWO
INTERRUPT

You can't change what you don't notice.

This part of the journey is about creating space between stimulus and response, between history and habit, between who you were told to be and who you're becoming. Interrupting the pattern isn't about being perfect. It's about becoming present.

In these chapters, we'll explore what's really happening in those spiral moments—when you yell, shut down, freeze, or fall apart. You'll begin to understand your nervous system as a wise protector, not a problem. And you'll start to replace guilt with grace by learning how to pause, notice, and choose something new.

You'll also meet your storm. The chaos. The overstimulation. The emotional noise. But this time, you won't just get swept away. You'll find your anchor.

Interrupting is not about never spiraling again. It's about learning how to catch yourself—and come back.

Welcome to the pause that changes everything.

05 | YOUR BODY KNOWS THE PATTERN

"Your body isn't betraying you—it's remembering. And every time you pause, breathe, and choose differently, you're teaching it safety."
- Unknown

She was just asking for a snack, so why did my chest tighten like a warning bell?

It was 4:03 p.m.—that hour of the day where everything feels too loud and not enough all at once.

The dishes weren't done. Homework wasn't started. Her youngest had just spilled applesauce on the couch, again. And as she finally sat down, her daughter's voice rang out from the kitchen:

"Mom! Can I have a snack?" Just five words. Normal, expected. But something in her tensed up.

Her shoulders stiffened. Her jaw locked. And before she could stop it, her voice rose:

"Can I *please* just have one minute without someone needing something from me?!"

The silence that followed hit harder than her own words.

Her daughter looked down at the floor. The request vanished. So did the softness in the room. And that's when it clicked.

This wasn't about the snack. It wasn't even about the mess or the noise.

It was about the way her body had braced—as if her daughter's voice was a threat, not a question. The way her nervous system had responded was like a fire alarm, not a doorbell.

You see, her body wasn't reacting to *now*...it was reacting to *then*.

To the childhood moments when asking for something—even something small—felt like a risk. When neediness was met with scorn. When being "too much" got you shut down, shamed, or sent away.

Her body had learned that requests were burdensome. That being needed meant being overwhelmed. That if she didn't overperform, she'd be overpowered.

She remembered one afternoon—she was nine, sitting cross-legged on the living room floor with her math homework spread out in front of her. The numbers were starting to blur as she tried solving the same word problem thrice, yielding the wrong answer each time. Her throat tightened as she looked up at her dad, who was home early for once, watching the news on the couch.

"Hey Dad, can you help me with this part?"

He didn't even look up.

"You need to learn how to problem solve on your own because I won't always be around," he mumbled. "Figure it out."

The rejection landed hard. It wasn't just about the homework. It was the message underneath:

Don't bother me. Handle it yourself. You're on your own.

She sat back down, heart racing. No more questions. No more trying. She scribbled something down just to finish it, blinking away the tears forming in her eyes.

It wasn't a loud moment. He didn't yell. He didn't call her names. But her body heard it clearly: *Needing help is annoying. Wanting a connection is too much. Get it right on your own, or not at all.*

And now, decades later, even a small request from her child—*Can you help me tie this? Can you show me again?*—made something old in her body tense and pull back.

Not because she didn't love them, but because her nervous system had equated need with failure. Asking for help still carried the old weight: *You should already know. You should do it yourself. You should be fine.*

It was never "just" about being triggered. It was her body doing what it had always done—protecting her from what it *used* to mean when someone needed her.

The raised voice, sharp tone, flood of irritation—those weren't personality flaws. They were survival codes, signals her nervous system had internalized long before she had the words to describe them.

And that's the part most of us miss when we try to "fix" our reactions: we forget that our bodies don't operate on logic. They operate on memory. Not the kind you can always recall, but the kind your muscles, breath, and heartbeat remember for you.

That moment reminded me of something I'm still learning to honor: **Your body will often remember what your mind has worked hard to move on from.**

And until you can slow down and listen to it, you'll keep reliving reactions that were never about the present moment to begin with.

There is power in the space between what just happened and what you do next.

For many of us, that space feels impossibly small. Maybe even nonexistent.

Your child spills the juice, sasses you, slams the door—and you've snapped before you even realize what's happening. You're yelling. Or shutting down. Or over-explaining. Or escaping into silence.

It happens so fast that the shame rushes in just as quickly.

"Why did I do that again?"

You know what kind of parent you want to be. You've read the books. You've done the work. And yet—here you are again. Reacting. Spiraling. Feeling like you failed.

But what if this isn't a failure?

What if it's your body remembering something you never got the chance to process?

This chapter is about reclaiming that tiny but powerful space before the reaction. Not through pressure or guilt. But through compassion and understanding.

Because when you pause, you don't just interrupt a reaction—you open the door to a new reality.

Let's practice slowing down. You're safe to do so now.

Let's start with a moment you probably know well.

You're standing in the kitchen. The clock is ticking toward dinner. Everyone's hungry. One child is melting down. Another is asking questions. There are dishes everywhere. And suddenly, someone yells, drops something, or talks back.

You feel it before you even think it.

Your heart pounds. Your stomach drops. Your jaw clenches. Your voice gets sharper before your brain can catch up.

And afterward, you feel that familiar shame ripple through you. *"Why did I do that?" "I knew better." "I promised I wouldn't yell again."*

This is where we pause the scene.

Not to critique. Not to correct. But to *zoom in*.

Because the moment you reacted? It wasn't a conscious choice. It was your nervous system following a well-worn path.

Your body knew the pattern.

Your reactivity isn't a flaw. It's a memory.

Not a memory in the way we think of stories or events, but a *body memory*—an imprint.

Your nervous system learned long ago what safety felt like. And what it didn't.

So, when your child slams the door, your body may not just be responding to the sound—it may be remembering the shouting you grew up with. When your child cries loudly, your tight chest might not mean you're frustrated—it might mean your body remembers that emotions weren't safe in your childhood home.

These reactions are not irrational. They are wired. Practiced. Familiar.

And that's the point: you're not failing. You're *remembering*.

Your body isn't trying to sabotage you. It's trying to protect you.

It's scanning for cues. It's reading between the lines. It's acting before your brain has a chance to step in.

Because when your nervous system perceives a threat—even an emotional one—it moves fast. Faster than your conscious thoughts.

This is what we mean when we say: the moment you react isn't the moment you choose.

Let me tell you a story.

A mother I worked with came to me in tears. "I keep yelling," she said. "I don't want to. I tell myself every day I'm going to stay calm. But then something happens, and it's like I black out. It's automatic."

We slowed down one of those moments together.

She described her child refusing to brush his teeth, shouting, "You can't make me!"

And instantly, she had grabbed his arm, her voice sharp, her body tense.

As we traced the scene, I asked her to pause—not on what she *did*, but what she *felt*.

She blinked. "I felt helpless. Out of control. Like he had the power."

We traced that feeling back. To moments where she felt small. Ignored. Where no one cared what she needed, only how she behaved.

Her body wasn't reacting to the child in front of her.

It was responding to the child she used to be.

This is the heart of what I want to teach you:

Body before behavior.

Before you yell, freeze, or explain for the fifth time, your body has already decided: *This is familiar. This is a danger. I know what to do.*

But here's the good news: just as your body learned how to protect you, it can also learn how to pause.

The pattern isn't who you are. It's just what you've practiced.

And if you can practice panic, you can practice peace.

Let's begin with one powerful tool: *The Pause Practice.*

The Pause Practice:

1. **Notice**: "I feel the heat rising."
2. **Name**: "This is a nervous system response."
3. **Breathe**: One hand on your heart, one on your belly. Inhale slowly for 4 counts, then exhale for 4 counts
4. **Respond**: Ask yourself, "What does this moment actually need from me?"

It might need silence. It might need presence. It might need nothing at all—except for you to soften.

This is not about perfection. It's about interruption.

Because every time you notice the pattern without judging it, you build a little more space. And in that space, you make room for choice.

You can't control the first wave of reactivity. But you can learn to ride it.

You can choose to breathe. To pause. To parent from the present, not the past.

Let's bring this even closer to home.

Pick a moment that usually sets you off. Maybe it's bedtime. Maybe it's transition time—leaving the house, ending screen time. Maybe it's your partner dismissing your concerns, and you feel your whole body harden.

Track what happens inside you:

- What physical cue shows up first? (Jaw clenching? Tight chest? Cold hands?)
- What thought follows? ("They never listen to me." "This always happens.")
- What do you usually do next?
- What would you want to do if you felt safe enough to choose?

This is your *Activation Map*.

And the more familiar you get with it, the easier it becomes to interrupt.

Here's your gentle challenge this week:

Pick one part of your daily routine—morning chaos, afternoon transitions, bedtime struggles—and commit to inserting one pause.

Even if it's just five seconds.

Put your hand on your heart. Breathe. Say, "I'm allowed to pause."

Notice what happens.

At the end of the day, reflect:

- What did I feel?
- What shifted?
- What might I try tomorrow?

Let these **reflection prompts** guide you deeper:

- **What situations consistently pull me out of my calm?**
- **What am I usually feeling underneath my reactivity? (Helplessness? Disrespected? Fear?)**
- **What does my body do when it feels unsafe, and what might it do if it felt supported?**

Add this phrase to your toolkit: **"This is a pattern, not a personal failure."**

Because that's what this chapter is about:

Not fixing yourself. But *noticing*.

Not shaming your body. But *thanking* it for trying to protect you.

And then, offering your body—and your inner child—a new experience.

You are not broken. You are remembering.

And now you are rewriting.

It begins with the pause.

You're safe to begin now.

06 | UNDER THE GUILT IS JUST A WOUND

"Guilt is often the surface story. Beneath it is a younger version of you—hurt, unheard, and just trying to feel safe."
-Anonymous.

The cupcakes almost broke her.

It wasn't about the cupcakes. Not really.

But there she was, still in her work clothes, icing store-bought cupcakes in her dim kitchen because she hadn't had time to bake the homemade ones she promised for the class party. The frosting kept sliding. The sprinkles looked messy. She felt behind again, not just in this moment, but in *motherhood*.

Her daughter would still have a treat to share. The kids wouldn't care, but her chest ached with guilt anyway.

She kept picturing the smiling, unbothered moms from Instagram—perfect bento lunches, hand-lettered notes in backpacks, and somehow, clean counters. She thought about her own mom, too—the way nothing was ever out of place, the way love was performed through presentation, the way *good* meant *put together*.

And suddenly, it wasn't just about the cupcakes. It was about *not being enough*.

She blinked hard, holding back tears, realizing this wasn't even about her daughter. Her daughter would love her no less. She probably wouldn't even remember the cupcakes.

But *she* would.

Because the guilt she felt wasn't coming from her child—it was coming from the part of her still trying to earn love through performance. Through excellence. Through being the "ideal mom" who never dropped the ball, let anyone down, or needed a pass.

That part of her had been around for a long time.

She was the little girl who got praised for being mature, quiet, and helpful. Who was told "you're so responsible" when really, she was just scared to make a mistake. She learned early that approval came when she stayed in line. That love felt more secure when she was admirable, self-sufficient, and not a burden. No one had to say the words—her body heard them anyway: *Be easy to love. Don't need too much. Don't mess up.*

So she strived. She over-delivered. She stayed two steps ahead. She got straight A's, anticipated everyone's needs, made herself indispensable—and invisible.

Now, as a mother, that same part still whispers in her ear. *You should've planned better. You should've remembered. You should've done more.*

Even when her child isn't asking for more. Even when no one is blaming her. That's when the cycle sneaks in.

Because when perfection becomes the standard, *presence* becomes conditional. She's so busy trying to measure up that she misses the chance to truly connect.

Her child isn't asking for a flawless mother.

But the guilt she carries—the guilt that flares when she rests, when she sets a boundary, when she simply forgets—it reveals a deeper wound:

The part of her that still believes love has to be earned...even in her own home.

She sat down at the kitchen table, the icing still uneven on the last row of cupcakes. Her hands were tired. Her heart even more so.

This time, she didn't push through. She didn't keep performing.

Instead, she paused while taking a deep breath and placed the spatula down. She whispered—more to herself than anyone else—*This doesn't make me a bad mom. I'm allowed to be enough without proving it every second.*

It wasn't some big, movie-like breakthrough, but it was real. It was resistance. It was repair.

Because when she stopped trying to meet the standard in her head, she finally made space to meet the child right in front of her.

The cupcakes were never the problem.

The deeper truth? Guilt had become her measuring stick. And perfection was how she tried to prove her worth.

There's something uniquely painful about guilt in motherhood—it doesn't just knock at the door, it barges in with a suitcase full of *shoulds*, a megaphone of self-criticism, and a high-definition reel of all the moments you wish you could do over.

Like the time you raised your voice—*again*. Or when your child needed patience and you had none left to give.
When you scrolled on your phone to escape.
When you said "I'm fine" but weren't.
When you went to bed feeling like the messiest version of yourself had taken the lead...and no one voted her in.

Or how about, when you handed them the iPad, not because it was best, but because you were bone-tired and had nothing left to give. Or when you have the day on a loop, replaying it and silently tallying up all the ways you feel you came up short.

And the hardest part?
It's not just the guilt in the moment—it's the fear of what it *might mean*.
That you're messing them up. That you're becoming the very parent you swore you'd never be.
That maybe you *are* too much. Or not enough. Or both, somehow, at the same time.

But here's what I've come to believe:
Guilt isn't the end of the story. It's the start of a conversation.

The beginning of the unveiling of something deeper than what meets the eye.
One that doesn't shame you, but helps you get curious. Because underneath the guilt, there's always something else.

A moment when your need was ignored.
A memory where you learned that being "too much" meant being rejected.
A belief you internalized that love had to be earned by being quiet, good, or perfect.

And although there might be this strong inclination to rid yourself of guilt, it's not a sign that something's wrong with you. It's a signal that something in you is still hurting and needs tending to—not a bandage, but a gentle, sustained kind of care—the kind that listens, honors, and makes space for healing at the root.

Because one thing guilt is not going to do is lead you to lasting change, because guilt will always come quickly, but it rarely stays long enough to teach you anything true.

One second you're overwhelmed, triggered, flooded with stress—and the next, you've snapped. You've raised your voice. You've shut down. You've slammed the cabinet just a little too hard.

And then... the guilt drops in.

That hollow, burning feeling in your chest. That inner voice whispering, *"You're ruining them."*

You replay the moment again and again, looking for the part where you could've stopped yourself. Where you could've paused. Responded differently. Been better.

But here's something no one told you:

That guilt you feel? It's not proof you're a bad mom.

It's evidence that your heart is deeply invested in getting it right, even when you feel like you're getting it wrong.

Because underneath the guilt is a wound. A place where your own needs were unmet. A place where you were expected to hold everything together and never fall apart. A place where you learned that love meant silence, that patience meant perfection, and that your emotions had to be swallowed whole.

So when you lose it now, not because you want to, but because your body can't hold it all anymore, what rises first isn't failure.

It's memory. It's grief. It's pain.

And that's the moment we begin with. Not to shame you. But to meet you there, with gentleness. Because the truth is: you don't need to parent from pain anymore.

You get to heal. You get to return. You get to lead with softness, even after the storm.

Let's tell the truth about guilt.

It's loud. It's sticky. It can feel like a verdict, like evidence in the courtroom of motherhood that you're failing.

But what if guilt isn't always a warning sign? What if it's a mirror?

What if the voice saying, "You're not enough," is actually revealing an old survival script? One you didn't choose—but one that shaped how you show up now?

Here's what I want you to hear:

Guilt doesn't always mean you did something wrong. Sometimes, it means you bumped into a part of you that still doesn't believe she's allowed to be human.

This is where we begin. Not with the behavior. But with the belief underneath.

Let's break down what really happens in those moments you feel ashamed of:

A trigger—something small but sharp: a spilled cup, a whiny tone, a defiant stare.

Your body tightens. Your breath shortens. Your heart races.

And before you even register it, you snap. Or you shut down. Or you over-accommodate just to make it all stop.

Then comes the shame. Then the guilt. Then the spiral:

Trigger → Reaction → Guilt → Shame → Overcompensate → Resentment → Repeat

But here's the missing piece: the reaction didn't come from who you are—it came from where you're still wounded.

It came from a nervous system that learned, long ago, that the safest way to survive was to yell, freeze, fawn, or flee.

You didn't fail because you reacted.

You reacted because you're still healing.

And the guilt you feel afterward? It isn't confirmation that you're broken.

It's your inner child whispering, *"I never learned how to be with this kind of discomfort."*

She wasn't taught how to be safe in the presence of big feelings—hers or anyone else's. So she panics. She tries to fix. She runs. She pleases. She lashes out.

But that's not who you are. That's who you had to be.

Now, we pause. Now, we listen. Now, we ask: *What if this guilt is just grief?*

Grief that no one made space for your hard days. Grief that you were never taught you could be imperfect and still be loved. Grief that being a "good girl" meant being invisible.

So many of us carry invisible rules we didn't choose. Beliefs about what it means to be a good mother. A good woman. A good person.

And these rules sound like:

- *"I should always be patient."*
- *"If they're upset, I've failed."*
- *"I'm not allowed to need space."*
- *"If I set a boundary, I'm being mean."*

But here's the truth:

Good is not perfect.

Good is present.

Good is honest.

Good is willing to repair.

Let go of the myth that your kids need a flawless mother.

They need a human one. One who feels. One who messes up. One who comes back with softness and says, "Let's try again."

Every time guilt rises up, ask yourself gently: *What am I afraid this moment means about me?*

Because guilt rarely shows up alone.

It travels with fear. With grief. With a deep ache for connection, safety, and worthiness.

Beneath your guilt might be a story like:

- "If I mess this up, they won't feel safe."
- "If I take space for myself, I'm neglecting them."
- "If I lose my temper, I've undone all my progress."

But those aren't truths. They're inherited beliefs. They're scripts written by a world that demanded mothers be martyrs and children be mirrors.

The next time you feel guilty, try this:

Pause.
Place your hand on your chest. And ask: "What part of me is hurting right now?"

Because guilt isn't just a feeling, it's a flag. A flare.
A signal from a part of you that still believes love has to be earned.

You begin to break the cycle when you see that part, not with shame, but with tenderness.

Your kids don't need you to be guiltless.
They need you to be curious.

To ask:

What is this really about?

Where did I learn this guilt?

What if I could offer myself understanding instead of judgment?

Because when you lead with curiosity instead of criticism, everything softens.

You learn to recognize:

This isn't just about the spilled milk.

It's about how I wasn't allowed to spill anything growing up.

It's about how I was taught to clean up everyone else's messes while hiding my own pain.

And in that moment of awareness? You create space.

Space to breathe. To choose. To respond—not from the wound, but from your wisdom.

This is where real change begins. Not in perfection. In presence.

If you take nothing else from this chapter, take this:

You will mess up.

You will yell.

You will forget to breathe.

You will parent from pain sometimes.

That's not the end of the story. That's just the middle.

Because real magic doesn't live in perfect responses. It lives in *repair*.

When you circle back, even after a hard moment, and say:

"I'm sorry I yelled. That wasn't your fault. I was overwhelmed—and I'm working on that."

You are doing what many of us have never experienced. You're modeling accountability. You're creating emotional safety. You're showing your children that relationships can bend without breaking.

Repair isn't a weakness. It's a strength. It teaches your children that love isn't destroyed by rupture—it's *deepened* by return.

When they see you own your missteps, they learn they don't have to hide theirs. They learn that mistakes are part of love. That perfection isn't the standard—presence is.

The Guilt Mirror Practice

When guilt visits you—and it will—try this five-step reflection:

1. **What happened?**
   What triggered the moment? What was going on around you?
2. **What am I feeling guilty about?**
   Get specific. Is it yelling? Shutting down? Not being "enough"?

3. **Whose voice is this guilt speaking in?**
   Is it yours? Or does it sound like a caregiver, a cultural message, an old script?
4. **What is this guilt pointing to beneath the surface?**
   What fear or wound is it connected to?
5. **What do I need right now?**
   What would bring relief? A breath? A break? A word of reassurance?

You can even whisper:

"This is not who I am—it's what I've been through."
"This is not a verdict—it's an invitation."

And that invitation is always this: To come home. To choose presence. To offer compassion to yourself first, so you can offer it freely to them.

Let's name something that might feel radical:

You don't have to be fully healed to be a safe, loving, and incredible mother.

You just have to be aware and willing.

Because parenting while healing is messy. It's brave. It's sacred.

You're doing something generations before you couldn't or didn't have the tools to do. You're choosing to stay soft where you were once hardened. You're choosing to speak what was once swallowed. You're choosing to pause when your body wants to repeat the pattern.

That's not failing. That's rising. And every time guilt tries to pull you back into shame, you now have a different path.

You can say:

"I'm not a perfect mom. I'm a present one." "I'm not parenting from pain anymore. I'm parenting from awareness." "I'm not the mother I was yesterday—and that's proof I'm growing."

The next time you feel the pull of guilt, try this:

Don't push it down.

Don't spiral with it.

Don't wear it like a label.

Instead, get curious.

And reflect with these prompts by asking:

- What is this guilt really about?
- What story is it trying to tell me?
- What part of me is asking to be seen, soothed, and supported?

You don't have to carry the weight of every mistake.

You just have to keep showing up with softness.

You just have to keep coming back.

Because the legacy your children inherit won't be written in your guilt.

It will be written in your returns. Your repair. Your honesty. Your willingness to say, "I'm learning, and I love you."

And that? That's what makes you safe. That's what makes you enough. That's what makes you whole.

Closing Journal Prompt

If I believed guilt was a wound, not a verdict, how would I show up for myself next time I mess up?

Let that be your anchor.

Let that be your pause.

Let that be the beginning of a new story.

07 | FINDING STILLNESS IN THE STORM

"He will cover you with His feathers, and under His wings you will find refuge; His faithfulness will be your shield and rampart."
— **Psalm 91:4**

She didn't yell, and she didn't smile through it either.

It was getting late into the evening, and everything was falling apart.

The toddler was wailing because she got the wrong color cup. The older one was pacing the kitchen, asking questions faster than she could answer them. Something was burning in the oven. The dog was barking at absolutely nothing. And somehow, everyone needed something at once.

She felt the familiar surge rising in her chest—the heat behind her eyes, the tightness in her shoulders, the buzzing panic that told her to snap, yell, and *fix it all right now*.

This used to be the moment she'd lose it.

She'd shout. Slam a cabinet. Guilt would hit instantly, but not fast enough to stop the damage. Her nervous system had always gone from calm to chaos in two seconds flat, and she thought that was just who she was: *reactive, high-strung, too much.*

But this time was different.

...She inhaled slowly, letting the noise swirl around her while she stayed right where she was. One hand on her heart. One breath. Then another.

Not to fix anything. Not to make the kids quiet. Just to stay with *herself*.

A quiet sentence surfaced, one she'd practiced whispering when it all got too loud: *I can be safe in my body, even if the room isn't calm.*

The toddler was still crying. The questions kept coming. The kitchen was still chaos, but she was no longer bracing against it.

She hadn't always known how to do this.

The shift came months earlier, after a night she still winces to remember—when she had screamed at her kids so loudly the baby started crying harder, and her older child quietly asked, *"Are you mad at me, or just everything?"* That question broke something open in her.

She had spent years white-knuckling her way through motherhood, hoping the next routine, planner, or podcast would give her the peace she was chasing, but nothing worked for long.

The real cost was her kids flinching at her tone. Her own body living in a constant state of tension. The shame that followed every blowup. She finally realized: calm couldn't be something she waited for—it had to be something she *practiced*.

And now, with this small pause—hand to heart, breath in, breath out—she could feel the shift.

Not fixing everything. Not getting it all right. Just staying with herself.

But fewer apologies. More connection. Moments where her kids leaned in instead of away. Moments where she didn't have to recover, because she never exploded in the first place.

She wasn't calm because the world was quiet. She was calm because her body remembered how to anchor itself, even in the storm.

And that changed *everything*.

She didn't need silence to find stillness. She didn't need her kids to regulate so she could. She had learned that calm wasn't something you waited for. It's something you *build*.

This mama's story taught me something I carry into every other area of my life, especially motherhood: You can feel overwhelmed and still be held. You can feel stretched and still be sustained. And you don't have to carry the storm alone when you know where to run for shelter.

You also don't need to flee the storm to find your shelter.

You don't need a yoga retreat, a quiet cabin in the woods, or a therapist's office with soft lighting and gentle music. You also don't need everyone to behave, the house to be quiet, or the schedule to go according to plan.

What you need is something real. Something reachable.

Tools that work *in the moment*—not when the world pauses, but while life is still moving. Not when everything aligns, but when it all falls apart.

Tools that help you return to your center *while* the storm is swirling around you.

Now, I want to pause here and acknowledge something important: this chapter isn't about striving for perfection. I know that being told to "just be calm" can feel frustrating, even dismissive.

For so many mothers---especially those trying to break generational cycles---it can land like another impossible standard to meet. Another way to fall short. Because for so many of us, "calm" starts to sound like code for "never lose it." "Always be composed." "Don't feel too much. Don't mess up."

I get it if the word *calm* has felt heavy or unrealistic to you. I've felt that, too.

But that's not what I mean by calm. Not here.

In this chapter, calm isn't about suppressing emotion, silencing your anger, or pretending to be serene when you're actually unraveling inside. It's not about being unfazed, unbothered, or unbreakable. It's about finding your footing *while* things feel wobbly.

It's about discovering an inner anchor---not because you should, but because you *can*.

Because calm isn't a personality trait. It's a *practice*. You have permission to start over, right where you are.

Let's begin with a moment from my own life.

There were days I felt like I couldn't catch my breath. Motherhood was loud, relentless, and overstimulating—and I didn't always have the time or space to do the things that calmed me most.

So, I learned to steal little pockets of calm.

I made my favorite tea and actually tasted it. I became intentional about what I let play on the radio—something that made me feel light, not drained. And when it got to be too much? I stepped outside.

Nature became my reset. A walk, even just five minutes in the sun, reminded my body that it was safe to slow down—that my nervous system didn't have to live on high alert.

I didn't need everything to be quiet around me. I just needed to find quiet *within* me.

Let's talk about what's happening inside when you feel overwhelmed—the event that encourages the desire to escape, control, or shut down entirely.

Because overwhelm isn't just about what's *happening*—it's about what's *been held* for far too long.

Your nervous system kicks into protective mode when you're in a high-stress moment. This is often called "fight, flight, freeze, or fawn." It's not because you're weak—it's because your brain is wired for survival.

When your child starts screaming or your toddler throws food, your brain isn't scanning for logic. It's scanning for threats. It floods your system with stress hormones. Your heart rate quickens. Your breath shortens. Your thoughts race. You feel like you need to react now.

And this is *common*.

But this is also why you snap, why you shut down.
It is also why you feel like you're watching yourself from the outside, wondering, *Why am I doing this again?*

Your body is responding to perceived danger, even when you're "just" dealing with spilled milk.

The key isn't to avoid stress—it's to help your body feel safe in it.

This is what stillness means.

Not silence. But safety.

You see, Mama, we've been taught a lie.

That we can only feel peaceful when the environment is peaceful.

That calm happens *after* the tantrums end, the house is clean, *and* the kids go to sleep.

But that belief puts your peace in the hands of everyone else's behavior.

And let's be honest: with kids? That peace may never come.

Stillness is not about controlling the storm. It's about not joining it.

You can be in the middle of chaos and still access something solid inside you.

You can parent from a place of inner strength even when everything is loud.

Because stillness doesn't mean silence. It means you're connected to something deeper than the noise.

Let me share a story.

A mother I worked with used to spiral the moment things got chaotic. Her go-to was yelling—not because she wanted to, but because she didn't know another way to interrupt the tension.

Then she started practicing a simple ritual:

Hand on heart. Three slow breaths. One anchor phrase: *"I can be calm, even when it's loud."*

It took 15 seconds. But it changed everything.

The kids still fought. The noise was still there. But *she* was different.

And because she didn't escalate, neither did they.

She didn't need the chaos to stop in order to regulate. She needed to reconnect with herself.

Here's what I want you to know:

Your calm is contagious.

Your kids borrow your nervous system until they build their own.

They don't need you to be perfect. They need you to be a safe place to land.

And when your body is grounded, their bodies feel safer too.

This is co-regulation. This is nervous system leadership.
This is how you change the tone of your home without over-delivering by raising your voice.

She didn't get there overnight, and neither will you. But the beauty is—it's not about grand transformations. It's about small choices, in real moments.

The kind of moments where you're holding the baby on your hip, the dog is barking at the door, and your toddler is on the floor sobbing because their banana broke. You're overstimulated. Under-resourced. And all you want to do is scream—or leave.

This is when you need something simple. Something doable, and I call them Interrupt Rituals. Tiny, grounding practices that pull you back to yourself when everything else is pulling you away.

They don't require a lot. They don't need you to have a perfect plan. They just need repetition. And a little willingness to begin.

These rituals are like little lifelines—tucked into your day, ready to meet you mid-moment, without asking anyone else to change first.

They fit in your pocket. They don't demand stillness around you—only within you. And they remind you, gently, that you're allowed to be okay, even when things aren't.

So, what do these rituals actually look like? Let me show you what's worked for me—and for many other mothers learning to steady themselves in the chaos:

You might find yourself placing a hand on your heart, another on your belly, and taking a slow, intentional breath. That's a body-based cue.

Maybe you step outside for 30 seconds and let the air hit your face, or run cold water over your wrists—just enough to remind your body that you're safe. That's sensory-based regulation.

Or perhaps you whisper to yourself, *"This is a moment. Not a measure of my motherhood."* Or *"This is hard, but I'm here."* Lastly, *"I'm safe. They're safe. We'll get through this."* That's a mantra—words that anchor you when everything else feels unsteady.

These are just starting points. You'll find the ones that work for you. And when you do, you can stitch them together into your own go-to sequence for those high-stress moments.

We'll build it together. Slowly. Gently. One layer at a time.

Your Interrupt Ritual is like a personal pause button—a way to come back to yourself without needing to disappear.

Here's how you can begin to build your own:

1. Pick a grounding body cue. Place a hand over your heart. Shake out your arms. Choose a simple action that reconnects you to yourself.

2. Find a phrase that feels true. Choose words that anchor you in the chaos. Something like: *"This is not a crisis. This is just a hard moment."*
3. Choose a sensory anchor. A deep breath. A calming scent. A cool splash of water. Find something that signals to your body: *It's okay to settle.*

Then weave them together. Let it be yours.

When the moment swells and you feel yourself rising with it, pause. Breathe. Anchor.

Say your words out loud if you need to. Let them interrupt the spiral.

This is your reset. And the more you return to it, the more your body remembers: I'm not stuck in this pattern. I can choose differently.

Stillness isn't something you wait for. It's something you practice. Right here. Right now.

Let's reflect on this together for a moment. These aren't "assignments"—they're gentle invitations. Consider them quiet doorways into yourself:

- Can you remember the last time it all just felt like too much? What was happening—and what did you *really* need?
- What have you been reaching for when your body is shouting for a pause? A scroll? A snap? A shutdown?
- What small thing, no matter how simple, helps you feel just a little more anchored?
- What would it feel like to carry calm into the room... instead of waiting for the room to be calm first?

Let's make this real, together.

Pick one moment in your day that usually sends your nervous system into overdrive. Maybe it's the scramble before school. Or the whines at dinner. Or that endless stretch before bedtime.

That's your practice ground.

Use your Interrupt Ritual once—just once—in that zone today.

And then tonight, instead of replaying everything you "did wrong," ask yourself:

- Did I pause at all, even for a breath?
- What helped, even a little?
- What might I try differently next time?

This isn't about scoring yourself. It's about noticing. About learning what support actually feels like in your body. About offering yourself grace for being human, and brave for showing up anyway.

This is how you build trust in yourself.

Not by never getting triggered, but by learning to catch it sooner.

Not by eliminating chaos, but by creating calm inside it.

You deserve to feel safe. You deserve to feel steady. You deserve to pause—even when everything feels like it's falling apart.

You don't need to earn your peace by fixing everyone else first.

You are allowed to start with you.

Because when you return to yourself, you bring everyone else home too.

Let this reflection prompt stay with you:

What does stillness feel like for me, and how can I come back to it, even when everything else feels loud?

And let this be your reminder:

Stillness isn't out there. It's already in you.

Let's keep coming home to it—one breath, one moment, one rooted step at a time.

PART THREE
SHIFT

Now that you can see the pattern and pause the spiral, it's time to pivot.

In this part of the journey, you'll learn how to mother from your values, not your wounds. You'll start to replace old scripts like *"If I give more, they'll love me more,"* or *"If I say no, I'm mean,"* with grounded truths rooted in emotional safety, not performance.

These chapters will guide you through what it looks like to parent with calm leadership, clear boundaries, and emotional integrity. You'll practice saying no from love, not fear. You'll begin to let go of people-pleasing and overgiving. And you'll finally stop abandoning yourself in the name of being "a good mom."

Because your children aren't just learning what to do. They're learning how to be—how to feel, repair, and return to themselves.

And they learn it from you.

You are the model, the map, and the mirror. It's time to lead from the truth of who you are.

08 | YOU DON'T HAVE TO OVERGIVE TO BE A GOOD MOM

"Caring for yourself is not self-indulgence, it is self-preservation."
— **Audre Lorde**

The day I realized I was disappearing too.

I watched my mother give everything.

Not just the usual sacrifices—making sure we ate first, or staying up late to finish laundry. I mean *everything*. Her rest. Her boundaries. Her voice. She gave until there was nothing left but an outline of the woman she used to be.

As a child, I didn't understand it. I just knew she was always tired. Always busy. Always doing.

But now, as a woman and mother, I see it differently. I see how overgiving became her love language—how it made her feel needed, worthy, safe. I also see what it cost her.

She didn't get to have bad days. She didn't know how to say no without guilt. She didn't trust that her presence was enough without proving it through constant doing. And maybe the hardest part to admit? She never truly received because when you're always giving, you don't leave much room for being held.

That kind of caretaking looks noble on the outside—but inside, it's often just a survival strategy wrapped in praise.

Watching her, I internalized a message I didn't even know I was absorbing:

That to love well, you must *empty yourself*. That being tired all the time meant you were doing it right. That good mothers didn't need—they just gave.

So, I grew up equating love with self-neglect. I learned to be helpful, not honest. To anticipate others' needs before acknowledging my own. To see rest as laziness, and asking for help as weakness.

And for a while, it worked. People praised my selflessness. I became the dependable one. The strong one. The one who "had it all together," but inside, I was tired in a way that sleep couldn't fix.

It wasn't until I became a mother myself that I began questioning the story. Because as I watched my child look up at me—not for what I could *do*, but for who I *was*—I realized I didn't want to pass this version of love down another generation.

I didn't want them to think that being a "good" anything—mother, partner, friend—meant being everything to everyone at the expense of yourself.

So I started slow. I practiced saying, *"I'm tired."* I let myself sit down when the house was still messy. I asked for help, even when I felt guilty. I reminded myself that my worth was not measured by how depleted I was at the end of the day.

And here's what surprised me: The sky didn't fall. My children didn't love me less. The world didn't stop turning.

But I started returning to myself. And in that return, I found a new kind of motherhood. One rooted not in overgiving, but in presence. One where love wasn't something I had to prove through exhaustion, but something I could live from, freely and fully.

Picture this:

You've packed the lunches, handled the tantrum, planned the birthday party, cleaned up the spilled milk, stayed late to finish work, folded laundry at midnight—and still, you feel it:

That quiet ache whispering, *"It's not enough."*

That gnawing pressure, as if love had a checklist you're always just a few tasks behind on.

It's a cruel math, isn't it? No matter how much you give, the equation never balances.

Because you were taught that love = self-erasure. And that's where the ache really comes from.

Not from your lack. But from the belief that your worth is tied to your depletion.

Let's go back a bit.

Many of us grew up absorbing messages like:

- "A good mom puts herself last."
- "Rest is selfish."
- "Mothers are supposed to be tired—it means you're doing it right."

We watched women we loved and admired run themselves ragged, believing that sacrifice was synonymous with strength.

We learned to equate love with over-functioning. And in a way, it made sense.

Overgiving became a survival skill in a world that often didn't see the full humanity of women and mothers.

It was a way to be needed. To be valued. To stay connected.

But what once protected us is now breaking us.

And the very thing we want to pass down—presence, connection, emotional safety—can't survive if we're empty inside.

Let me share a story with you that brings home this point.

I remember working with a mom who was living this cycle daily.

She said yes to every request, favor, and need.

Her calendar was a tapestry of obligations she didn't even want.

And still, she lay awake at night, guilt gnawing at her: *Am I doing enough?*

One day, after yet another burnout crash, she sat with me and said, "I thought doing it all would make me a good mom. But I'm starting to realize… my kids don't need *all of me gone*. They need *me* to be present."

That was her turning point. Maybe today will be yours too.

Let's talk about the real difference between **performative giving** and **true nourishment**.

Performative Giving feels like:

- Saying yes when you want to say no.
- Smiling when you're breaking inside.
- Showing up out of guilt, fear, or pressure.
- Resenting the very people you love.

True Nourishment feels like:

- Showing up because you *choose* to.
- Setting boundaries without apology.
- Resting because your body deserves it, not because you "earned" it.
- Loving from a place of fullness, not depletion.

Here's a gentle truth:

You cannot model emotional regulation if you're emotionally starved.

Your kids feel your presence, but they also feel your burnout. They don't need you to give endlessly.

They need you to live honestly, and sometimes the most loving thing you can say to your children and yourself is "No."

No to overcommitting. No to resentment disguised as selflessness. No to betraying your own needs in the name of "being a good mom."

Because every "no" you offer from love creates room for a deeper "yes" to what matters most.

"No" teaches boundaries. "No" teaches respect. "No" teaches your children that they, too, are allowed to protect their peace.

When you honor your limits, you give your children permission to honor theirs.

This is emotional leadership. And it starts with you.

Here's the shift I want you to imagine:

Parenting from overflow, not obligation.

Imagine showing up to your life, not because you're running on fumes, but because you're nourished enough to *choose* it.

Imagine loving not from scarcity—"I have to, or I'm failing"—but from abundance:

"I have enough to share because I've filled my own cup first."

This is not selfish. This is sacred stewardship of your energy, your heart, your life.

Overflow is powerful. Obligation is exhausting. Which one do you want to live from?

If you're wondering how to start shifting, here's a small but mighty practice:

The Self-Check-In Before Saying Yes

When a request comes your way—big or small—pause.

Ask yourself:

- Am I saying yes to be loved, or because I want to?

- Am I betraying myself to meet someone else's expectation?
- What would honoring myself look like here?

Then choose not from fear, but from self-trust.

And know this:

Every "no" rooted in self-respect is a "yes" to the life you're building. Every boundary you set plants a seed of safety for you and your children.

Here's something to reflect on:

- **What did I learn growing up about what it means to be a "good" mother?**
- **Where in my life am I overgiving out of fear or guilt?**
- **What would a nourished version of me choose instead?**

Let those questions marinate. Not to shame yourself, but to begin setting yourself free.

This week, try this: set **one small boundary**.

It could be tiny:

- "I'm not available after 8 PM."
- "I'm taking 10 minutes to myself before dinner."
- "I'm not adding one more thing to my plate this week."

And when you do, celebrate it! Not as rebellion, but as reclamation.

Every boundary you set honors the mother you are becoming. A mother who stays with herself. A mother who gives from wholeness, not wounds.

A mother who knows:

My worth isn't in what I do for others.

My worth is who I am—even when I rest, even when I pause, even when I say no.

Let's leave this chapter with one last reflection:

If I believed my worth didn't come from what I do for others, what would I stop doing today? What would I start giving back to myself?

Because love isn't measured by depletion, it's measured by presence.

And the greatest gift you can give your children is a mother who hasn't abandoned herself.

09 | LOVE DOESN'T ALWAYS SOUND LIKE YES

"Sometimes love says no, not to reject, but to protect."
— **Anonymous**

"Good mothers don't say no".

Sitting across from me, exhausted and on the edge of tears, she shared the moment she tried to protect her own energy—and immediately felt selfish for it, so she decided to give in instead.

The request came at the end of a long, frayed day: another five more minutes of play, but this time with mommy.

The logical part of her knew she was tapped out—bone tired, heart heavy, stretched so thin that even breathing felt like one more thing to manage, but the guilt in her chest was louder.

Her daughter stood there holding two Barbies, eyes bright with hope. So, she said yes. Again. Even though she didn't have it to give.

But her mind started spinning: *Don't ruin her night. Don't make her sad. She'll be mad. She won't understand. Don't be the reason she feels disappointed.*

All the pressure to be the "good mom," the "yes mom," flooded her chest like heat. She wasn't just reacting to her daughter but to something much older.

Because in her house growing up, "no" never meant safety. It meant disconnection. Rejection. Say no to your parents? You were punished. Isolated. Ignored. Yelled at.

Ask them for something and hear "no"? You learned quickly not to ask again. Boundaries weren't explained—they were enforced with silence or shame.

So she adapted. She became agreeable, easy. The one who didn't push, didn't need much, didn't say no because pleasing kept her close, and no meant loss.

And now, here she was—decades later—struggling to say no to her child because her body still remembered what "no" used to cost her.

And the message she gave her daughter that night was: if love costs you yourself, give more anyway, even when it hurts, even when you're empty, even when it's not true.

Later, as she lay awake replaying the day and thinking of a way to stop swallowing her needs or stretching past her limits, a quiet thought surfaced: *"If this is love... why does it feel like I'm abandoning myself?"*

It's a question many of us are afraid to ask. Because somewhere along the way, we learned to equate love with saying yes. To say no—to hold a boundary, to disappoint, to disrupt—felt like rejection. Like failure.

But real love, the kind that builds trust and security, doesn't always sound like yes. Sometimes, love sounds like a boundary. Sometimes, love sounds like *"no, not right now."* Sometimes, love sounds like holding steady while a child flails against the limits they desperately need but cannot yet articulate.

And that, mama, is not failure. It's emotional leadership.

Growing up, many of us received a confusing message: Approval felt like love. Compliance felt like safety. The path to connection was paved with yes after yes after yes.

Be easy. Be agreeable. Don't rock the boat. Don't risk rejection.

If you were loved, you were allowed to belong.

It makes sense, then, that as mothers, we fear that "no" will cost us closeness. That saying no to another bedtime story, another piece of candy, another demand, will be received not as a limit, but as withdrawal.

We learned early that making people happy kept us safe. But motherhood invites us into a different truth:

Real love isn't about keeping people happy. It's about keeping people safe—even when they're disappointed.

I once worked with a mother who came to me in tears. Always saying yes to everything, because she thought that's what good moms did.

Yes, to extra snacks even when dinner was ready. Yes to one more episode, even when it was time for homework to be completed. Yes, to fifteen more minutes of playtime, which really translates into a negotiation of extra time added, totaling an additional forty-five minutes earned.

And somewhere along the way, she disappeared.

Her yeses were not born from joy. They were born from fear of tantrums, rejection, and being "too much" or "not enough."

But what she didn't realize was that every exhausted yes, every resentful agreement, was teaching her children something too.

It was teaching them that love means ignoring your own needs. That connection requires self-erasure.

And that was not the legacy this mother wanted to leave.

Her turning point came quietly. It wasn't a major breakdown. It was a small, everyday moment—looking into her child's eyes after yet another half-hearted yes and realizing she wasn't truly there.

Her body was in the room, but her heart had left.

One night, worn thin, the mother tried something different.

When her daughter asked for a fourth book, she got on her daughter's level and said gently, "I love you so much. And tonight, we're reading two books. Then it's time to rest. It's okay if you feel sad about that. I'm here."

Her daughter wailed. Begged. Pushed.

And she stayed steady. She didn't yell. She didn't give in. She didn't shut down.

And after the tears? Stillness.

Her daughter crawled into her lap and fell asleep—deeply, peacefully.

What she needed wasn't another book. She needed the security of her mom's grounded leadership.

She realized something profound:

It wasn't saying yes that made her child feel loved. It was her steadiness. Her certainty. Her calm *"no"* was wrapped in an unwavering presence.

We often fear that setting boundaries will harm our connection with our children. But the opposite is true.

Boundaries **create** safety. Boundaries **build** trust. Boundaries *are* love.

A consistent limit held with warmth tells a child, *"You are safe here. You can push, protest, and be upset—and I will stay steady."*

It tells them: *"You are loved, even when you are disappointed."*

Boundaries aren't punishments. They're containers for growth.

They show children where their freedom lives—and where it meets reality.

When you say, *"I love you enough to say no right now,"* you teach them that love includes honesty, structure, and respect.

You don't need to armor up to say no. You don't need to over-explain, bribe, or plead. You don't need to defend your limits like they're courtroom arguments.

You can stay soft and firm. You can speak the truth and stay connected.

Here's a simple framework to help you:

The Calm "No" Framework:

- **Validate:**
  "I know you really want _____."
- **State the Boundary:**
  "And right now, the answer is no."
- **Anchor Safety:**
  "It's okay to feel disappointed. I'm here."

That's it. No lectures. No emotional withdrawal. Just presence and clarity.

And yes---it'll feel uncomfortable at first, but remember: discomfort isn't danger. Discomfort is growth.

And you can hold the line and hold their heart at the same time.

Inconsistent limits feel unsafe to children. When the rules shift based on your mood, their behavior, or your exhaustion, it creates a subtle anxiety:

"Can I trust the ground beneath me?"

They begin to test, not to be difficult, but to find the edges. To ask, in their own way, *"Are you strong enough to hold me through this?"*

They don't need a parent who says yes to everything. They need a parent who means what they say.

Predictability is safety. Consistency is trust. Clarity is love.

Each time you calmly hold a limit, you're building emotional infrastructure. Not a fortress. A home. A place where feelings are welcome. Where disappointment doesn't equal disconnection, where a no doesn't threaten love, it reveals it.

This week, I invite you to practice one calm "no."

Maybe it's bedtime.

Maybe it's one more snack.

Maybe it's an emotional moment where everything in you wants to give in because it's easier, but you choose to hold steady instead.

You don't have to be perfect. You don't have to get it right every time.

And when the protest comes—as it might—stay grounded. Stay kind. Stay present.

Remember: you're not raising a child who never hears no. You're raising a child who can feel safe inside it.

Because every time you stay steady when they feel wobbly, they learn something profound:

That love isn't earned by compliance. That boundaries don't threaten connection. That they can handle disappointment—and so can you.

You are not selfish for needing space. You are not cruel for saying no. You are not unloving for holding a line. You are wise. You are steady. You are rewriting a legacy.

Because your child doesn't need a parent who disappears into their yeses, they need a mother who can be trusted to be real. A mother who doesn't abandon herself to keep the peace. A mother who shows them: *"I will not crumble when you are upset."* Love that bends in every direction to avoid conflict teaches fragility.

And love that roots in clarity and stays kind? That teaches strength.

You're building emotional muscle every time you say "no" with calm, compassion, and consistency. For them. And for you.

And over time, they won't remember every denied snack or delayed screen. They'll remember your steadiness, your safety, and your ability to stay soft and sure at the same time.

Closing Reflection

You are not raising a child who will never feel disappointment.
You are raising a child who knows they are loved, even when they hear no.

That's real security. That's love that lasts.

So ask yourself:

- **Where do I say yes when I really mean no?**
- **What am I afraid will happen if I disappoint them?**
- **What if my calm, grounded no is the most loving thing I could offer?**

You are not less loving for setting boundaries.

You are more trustworthy. More rooted. More free.

Because love doesn't always sound like "yes."

Sometimes, it sounds like: "I'm here. I see you. And I'm holding the line—because you, and I, are both worth protecting."

10 | THEY LEARN TO FEEL FROM YOU

> *"Children are great imitators.*
> *So, give them something great to imitate."*
> **— Anonymous**

She didn't mean to pass down her pain, but he was already carrying it.

Not through lectures. Not through punishment. But through the way her eyes darted toward messes like they were emergencies. Through the way she flinched at loud noises. Through the way she rushed to clean up toys *before* the company arrived, snapping at him with a tight jaw and a forced smile.

Through the way she apologized too much. Through the way she held her breath.

Her son was so little, but he had already started tiptoeing.

That morning, she caught him nervously watching her face after accidentally knocking over his cup of water. He froze, waiting, not for words, but for her energy. He didn't look at the mess. He looked at *her* because that's how he knew whether things were safe.

She hadn't yelled. She hadn't blamed him. She had even said, "It's okay, bud. We'll wipe it up."

But she saw the way his shoulders curled in, like he was already bracing for something he couldn't name. And that's when it hit her: *He's not reacting to the spill. He's reacting to how I feel about the spill.*

That moment was her wake-up call. Not because she had done something terrible. But because she saw how easy it is to pass down fear, not in what we say, but in how we *feel* out loud.

That urgency. That fear of messing up. That instinct to fix everything before someone got mad.

It was how *she* used to feel.

How she still felt, sometimes, when she dropped the ball or forgot something important.

Because growing up, mistakes weren't just corrected—they were punished, shamed, or used as proof that she wasn't trying hard enough. Like the time she was standing at the front of the classroom with her spelling test in hand. She had studied. She *thought* she'd done well. But when the teacher came over and quietly whispered, "Seventy-two. You're usually better than this," her stomach dropped. A few kids who overheard snickered. She nodded quietly, holding back tears, already promising herself it wouldn't happen again.

That day, she didn't just feel embarrassed. She felt unsafe.

She learned that mistakes were not just moments—they were marks on her worth.

So, she learned to scan, to soothe, to stay small. And even though she's grown now, her nervous system never forgot that lesson: *Don't fall short. Don't disappoint anyone. Love felt safest when she got everything right.*

She'd been working so hard to be a calm, fully aware, cycle-breaking mom. But he hadn't learned this from her discipline—he had learned it from her *discomfort with herself.*

He was learning that small mistakes carry big weight. That tension means something bad might happen. That love means keeping others comfortable, even when you're uncomfortable inside.

And none of that was what she wanted to teach him.

But this was her chance—not to be perfect, but to get present. To start healing out loud. To start saying, *"That startled me, but it's okay."* To show him what it looks like to take a breath, name a feeling, and stay connected.

Because if kids learn to tiptoe by watching us walk on eggshells, they can also learn to exhale by watching us come back to ourselves.

And this is the heart of it: Our children don't just hear what we say—they *feel* how we say it. They don't just follow our instructions—they absorb our emotional patterns. They learn from the tone, the tension, the pauses, and the recovery. And when our actions and emotions don't align with our words, what we *feel* will always win out.

And instead of learning emotional clarity, they learn emotional confusion.

Instead of learning that feelings are welcome, they learn that feelings must be hidden. Instead of learning that it's okay to make mistakes and come back together, they learn to either explode or shut down.

That phrase may have been meant to maintain authority, but what it often creates is distance. And in the long run, it can cost us connection, safety, and trust.

You are not just a parent. You are the emotional leader of your home.

But leadership doesn't mean dominance. It doesn't mean perfection. It means being the one who goes first—first to breathe, first to repair, first to pause and choose differently.

Emotional leadership is not about managing your child's every move. It's about modeling the emotional patterns you want them to internalize—not fear, but calm. Not chaos, but consistency. Not harshness, but presence.

And it begins with clarity. Emotional leadership is built on three foundational pillars that help you lead from your values instead of your reactions:

- **Clarity of values:** Knowing what truly matters to you in your parenting, not just what you want to avoid, but what you want to embody.

- **Consistency of presence:** Showing up with steadiness, even when life is messy, noisy, or overwhelming.
- **Commitment to repair:** Choosing reconnection over perfection—especially after the hard moments.

When you stand on these pillars, you stop reacting from old scripts and start responding from your core.

This chapter is an invitation to step into that role with confidence and clarity. Not because you'll always get it right, but because you're willing to keep coming back to your center.

Because the truth is this: your calm, not your control, is what sets the emotional tone of your home.

Picture this: your child melts down over a broken crayon.

Your instinct rises fast. You want to fix it. Quiet it. Stop the noise. Or maybe you want to snap, shout, or walk away altogether.

You feel the familiar pull between two old instincts—control the chaos or get swallowed by it.

But what if neither is the only way?

What if your ability to stay connected—not in control—is the medicine they need most?

Children don't just hear what we say. They *feel* how we say it. And more than anything, they *absorb* how we navigate emotions—ours and theirs.

Their nervous systems develop through co-regulation. That means they "borrow" our bodies to learn what safety feels like. They learn to feel by watching *how* we feel. They learn what's safe by watching how we respond to stress, disappointment, and mess.

So, when we meet their outbursts with panic, shutdown, or shame, they learn that emotions are dangerous.

But when we meet them with breath, presence, and repair, they learn something else: That emotion isn't the enemy. That struggle doesn't mean separation. They're still safe, loved, connected—even when it's hard.

And this is where your personal values come alive—not just on paper, but in the way you live and lead.

I once worked with a mom who described tantrums as emotional emergencies. Anytime her child cried, she jumped in to fix it. She offered snacks, distractions, and solutions. Anything to make the crying stop.

But what she slowly began to see was this: she wasn't just soothing her child—she was trying to silence her own discomfort.

Her child's big feelings were triggering *her* belief that something was wrong, that she wasn't doing enough, that she was failing.

When she learned to stay—not fix, not flee, just *stay*—the whole energy of her home shifted.

The tantrums didn't disappear. But the fear did.

And with that came space. Space for her child's feelings. Space for her own. Space for connection that didn't depend on peace, but created it.

Here's the truth: most of us were never taught:

Calm is contagious. So is chaos.

Emotions move like the weather. They sweep through a room, unspoken but deeply felt. They transfer—quietly, instantly—through body language, tone, breath. If your nervous system is sounding the alarm, your child's will echo it. But if your body sends even a flicker of steadiness—*even if you're trembling on the inside*—they start to borrow that signal. They learn from you that it's possible to come back to center.

This doesn't mean you need to be calm all the time. It means learning how to come back to calm *before* trying to lead someone else there. It means being the anchor, not because you never drift, but because you know how to return.

And that returning starts with naming a few quiet truths: What do you lead with? Empathy? Firmness? Softness? Clarity? What have you been sacrificing that can't be lost anymore—your sleep, peace, and emotional truth?

You are not here to stop the storm. You're here to remember: *you're not the weather—you're the center.*

Let me tell you how that can look, not just in theory, but in real, everyday moments—the ones where the voices are loud, the energy is high, and you're not sure which way is up.

It starts with something simple: a pause.

You catch yourself before the words rush out. You notice your body—tight shoulders, a shallow breath. That's your cue. You breathe. You place a hand on your heart. You change your environment for a true reset if you need to. Then, you come back to yourself.

You name the feeling—quietly or aloud. *"I'm feeling overwhelmed." "I'm frustrated."* And just like that, you've stepped out of the spin and into awareness.

Now with this awareness and chance to regroup, you face your child, not to fix everything, but to co-regulate because you had the chance to position yourself for success. You soften your shoulders. You lower your voice. You steady your posture. *You don't have to join the unraveling even if they're unraveling.*

And when the moment passes—and it always does—you show them what recovery looks like.

"That was hard. I got overwhelmed, but I'm here now. I didn't like how I handled that. May I have a do-over?"

This isn't perfection. This is presence. This is emotional leadership—*not by force, but by example.*

Take a breath for a moment. Let the noise of the day fade just a little.

Now imagine this: your home as a place where emotions are welcome, not feared. A place where being human is safe. What would it look like to lead with the kind of love that's rooted, not reactive?

You don't need a vision statement. But you do need to know what matters most to you. What values are quietly shaping how you show up? What do you want your children to absorb—not from your rules but your rhythms?

Maybe it's empathy. Maybe it's boundaries with kindness. Maybe it's less about doing it all and more about being fully here.

You might also notice the hard things that rise inside you when your child is overwhelmed. The old scripts that echo: *"You're too much." "Calm down now." "I can't handle this."*

They're not mistakes—they're invitations. Old scripts may echo, but they don't get the final say. And it doesn't have to be dramatic. It can start with something as small as this:

The next time your child unravels—

Pause. Feel your feet on the ground. Place a hand on your chest or your belly. Say softly, to yourself if not out loud: *"I am the center, not the storm."*

Then speak. Not with fear. With care. With clarity of who you want to be in this moment.

It might feel clumsy. It might not "work" right away. But that moment? That's emotional leadership in action. That's how the blueprint is drawn.

Later, when the house is quiet again, take a minute to reflect. How did that feel? What did your body need in that moment? Where did your strength surprise you? Where did your tenderness show up?

It's not perfection that shapes them—it's what they see you practice. About what your children will carry—not word for word, but cell by cell, in their nervous system:

"When things got hard, my mom stayed."

Before we close, come back to this one reflection:

What kind of emotional world am I building for my children to live inside of?

Every breath you take, every boundary you hold with kindness, every time you choose to stay instead of shut down—that's the legacy.

Because the legacy you leave won't be in the rules you enforce. It will live in the safety you create.

You don't have to do it perfectly. You just have to stay present enough to say:

"This is hard. And we're safe inside it."

Your calm is the blueprint. Your presence is the medicine. Your leadership is the legacy.

And every time you breathe, ground, and stay, you're giving them something beautiful to imitate.

PART FOUR
EMBODY

This is where it all lands—in your body, breath, and being.

You've done the deep reflection. You've paused the patterns. You've shifted your responses. Now, you step fully into the identity of the calm, conscious, connected mother you've been becoming all along.

Embodying the work doesn't mean you'll never get triggered. It means you know how to return. How to reset. How to lead from your center, not your edge.

These final chapters are your homecoming. They're the story your children will remember—not just in words, but in the emotional atmosphere you've created. The way you show up. The way you circle back. The way you love them, even in the hard moments.

This is where legacy lives.

Not in what you leave behind—but in how you show up now.

Let's come home to that mother. She's been waiting for you.

11 | THE STORY THEY'LL REMEMBER STARTS HERE

> *"Children may not remember what you said, but they will never forget how you made them feel."*
> — **Adapted from Maya Angelou**

Dinner was done. Dishes are still in the sink. And then came the question that stopped me.

It wasn't a big moment. No special occasion. No milestone. Just a Tuesday night, after dance practice.

Dinner had ended, and the dishes were still piled in the sink. I was mentally checking out—exhausted from a long day, bracing myself for the bedtime routine. Then I saw my child curled up on the couch, clutching her favorite blanket, eyes tired but heart still wide open.

She didn't ask for anything dramatic. Just: "Will you sit with me for a few minutes?"

Part of me wanted to say no. (I wanted my own "me time"). I wanted quiet, space, and the comfort of collapsing or disappearing for a bit. Five minutes felt small. Easy to skip.

But something deeper nudged me: *This is the moment she'll remember.* Not what we ate. Not what I crossed off my to-do list, but whether I showed up.

So, I sat. No phone. No multitasking. Just being present.

She leaned into me with the kind of ease that only comes from feeling safe. Her little body softened as she let out a breath, and then—something shifted. The silence cracked open, and suddenly, it poured out:

The classmate who made her laugh. The moment at recess when she and her bestie had a disagreement. The part of dance practice she was nervous about, but proud that she tried anyway.

Things I would've missed if I had said, "Not now."

She opened the floodgates of her day—not because I asked, but because I paused long enough for her to know I was available to receive it. That moment of simple connection became her space for release, celebration, and being seen.

And I couldn't help but remember a time from my own childhood, just one of many moments when my parents felt fully *with* me.

I don't remember what we were wearing. I don't remember what day it was, but I remember sitting in the car with my dad, radio off, no rush. I had just had a hard day, and instead of fixing it, he just sat quietly, listening. Undistracted. Attentive without hovering. Fully invested in me.

The part that stood out to me the most was that he never minimized my concern. What may have been considered small to most was big enough for me, and knowing that I was free to vent about my hard math test was a quiet kind of comfort I didn't know I needed.

He didn't rush me past my feelings or try to talk me out of them—he just made space.

And in that space, I felt like I mattered because I was worth listening to. Even now, I remember how safe that felt.

And I realized—*this is what I'm passing down.*

Not perfect routines, screen-free dinners, or expert parenting techniques, but my presence without conditions. Moments when love didn't need to be loud—just available.

This is the story being written. Not the holidays or the family photos or the well-crafted birthday parties. But this—the quiet rhythms, the way love *feels* in the room, and their safety in being vulnerable.

That five minutes won't show up on a calendar, but it imprinted something.

And someday, when they look back on their childhood—not just the facts, but the *feeling*—**this** is what I hope they carry.

What if the legacy your children remember most isn't what you taught them, but how they felt in your presence, especially in the ordinary moments?

You've broken patterns. You've paused. You've healed parts of yourself you didn't even know were still hurting.

Now it's time to live the legacy you're creating. Not in grand declarations or rigid rules, but in small, sacred choices. The pause before you speak. The breath you take instead of yelling. The softness you extend to yourself after a hard day. These moments may feel ordinary, but they are not insignificant. They are your legacy in motion.

Legacy isn't something you leave behind. It's something you live with now.

Maya Angelou was right—your words may fade. But how do your children *feel* in your presence? That will echo through their nervous systems long after they've left your home. That is what becomes their emotional home base.

It begins with the values you define. It grows in the rhythms you repeat. And it lives on in the emotional atmosphere that your children will carry with them.

Because the truth is: you are not just breaking cycles. You are writing the emotional origin story your children will one day look back on.

Imagine this.

It's years from now. The dishwasher hums in the background. There's laughter at the table, the kind that comes after stories shared and bread broken. Your children—now adults—are sitting around, passing memories like bowls of food.

Someone leans back and says, "Remember when Mom..."

The sentence hangs there for a moment, like a breath waiting to be claimed.

What will they say next? What will they remember—not just about what you did, but about how they felt around you?

"She always had a soft place for us to land."

"She was strong, but she never made us feel small."

"She didn't get it right all the time, but we always knew we were loved."

"She always came back to us, even after she messed up."

This is the story you're writing. Right now. In the thick of the tantrums, the bedtime chaos, the constant backtalk, the whispered apologies at night when the house finally stills.

This---not control, image, or constant harmony- builds generational safety.

A common myth about legacy is that it's something lofty and far-off. Something sculpted in one grand moment of parenting greatness. The birthday parties. The vacations. The milestone wins. But that's not how it works.

Legacy lives in the way you set down your phone and look into your child's eyes when they ask for the fifth time. The way you circle back after conflict. It's in the breath you take when your body wants to yell. It's in the softening of your tone after a long, impossible day.

It lives in your rhythm. Your repair. Your return.

You may not always notice these moments. They may slip by unnoticed, uncelebrated. But your child notices. And long after the moment passes, the memory remains.

Not as a snapshot, but as a feeling.

They won't always remember what you said. But they'll remember how you made them feel. The story they'll remember is written in repetition. Not perfection.

You may have once believed that "doing it differently" meant being "on it" with minimal mishaps. But real healing doesn't look like constant calm or perfect routines.

Sometimes, it looks like locking yourself in the bathroom just to cry in peace. Sometimes, it's collapsing into bed at 8 p.m. because you've held too much for too long.

But healing also looks like returning. It looks like saying, "I'm sorry," without shame. It looks like showing up with a willing heart, not flawless performance---because grace meets us in the mess.

Every time you do, you're not just parenting—you're rising, rewriting, and showing your children what healing in real time looks like.

You're offering your children a blueprint for how to show up when things are hard. How to stay, even when it's messy. How to offer grace when emotions get loud.

Once, a mother that I had the pleasure of working with shared how she felt as if she was drowning in the chaos of parenting. Her daughter was fiery, sensitive, and unpredictable. Most days felt like walking through emotional landmines, with her evenings feeling heavy and her nights restless.

This mother started something small. Each night before bed, she asked one question: "What felt hard today?"

At first, her daughter gave silly answers. Or shrugged.

But she kept asking.

Over time, her daughter began to open up. To reflect. To cry sometimes. To ask her the same question in return.

What began as a five-minute practice became a nightly ritual. What started as a strategy became a portal to connection.

That's legacy.

Let's be honest—many of us were raised in homes that prized performance over presence.

- "Be good."
- "Don't cry."
- "Keep it together."

That's what was passed down.

But you get to build something different.

A performance legacy says, "She did everything. She never rested. She was always busy."

An emotional legacy says, "She heard me. She came back. She held space for me."

Which one are you building?

Which one do you want them to carry?

Legacy doesn't have to be elaborate. In fact, the most powerful rituals are often the smallest.

- A breath before you speak.
- A phrase you return to: "Let's reset."
- A boundary that says, "I love you enough to be clear."
- A daily check-in: "What was the best and hardest part of your day?"

Allow yourself to embody this concept by choosing 3–5 small actions that reflect who you are and who you're becoming. Let them guide you—not as a checklist, but as a compass.

Here's your invitation to live out your legacy.

Complete this sentence:

"The story I want to leave in my children's hearts is…"

Write it down. Post it somewhere visible. Let it remind you not of what you haven't done but what you're already creating.

You might not always see the fruit right away. But your child notices the pause. The softness. The consistency. The presence that comes not from being perfect, but from being present.

You are already shaping the story they will one day tell. And it won't be about whether you made Pinterest lunches or had a spotless home.

It will be about whether they felt safe. Whether they felt seen. Whether they knew love lived in the small moments, especially the hard ones.

Before we close the doors on this chapter, I'd like you to join me in a quick reflection.

If the story they remember started today…What would you want them to feel? How can you embody that now, even imperfectly?

It doesn't matter how the last chapter ended. What matters is the choice you make now.

Legacy is not fixed. It is flexible. Rewritable. Forged one moment at a time.

Begin again. Again and again. Every choice to return, every breath before the storm, every repair after the rupture—it all counts.

This isn't just parenting. It's soul work—real and lasting.

Let it be rooted in grace, guided by truth, and reflective of God's love through you.

12 | THIS IS WHAT COMING HOME FEELS LIKE

> *"She is clothed with strength and dignity;
> she can laugh at the days to come."*
> **— Proverbs 31:25**

No one saw what happened on the hallway floor that night, but she'd remember it for the rest of her life.

I consider it a calling and a deep honor to walk alongside the women I serve—holding space for their stories, trusting that God placed me here not just to listen, but to reflect His love, hope, and healing in the process.

I don't take this work lightly and celebrate their imperfectly perfect wins as we both bear witness to the transformation that unfolds when a woman begins to trust herself, honor her story, and show up with grace in the everyday moments.

And that is exactly what I got to experience with one of my mamas as she shared a simple, tender moment that became a turning point—not because her circumstances changed, but because something within *her* did.

She told me it happened in the middle of folding laundry.

She wasn't trying to have a breakthrough. It was just one of those long days—kids finally asleep, the house finally quiet, and there she was, surrounded by socks that didn't match and shirts stained with jelly. She was doing what so many mothers do: the invisible work that no one sees but everyone relies on.

At first, she felt that familiar resentment start to bubble up.

Why is this always mine to carry?

Why does no one notice what I do?

Why am I always the one holding everything together, even when I feel like I'm falling apart?

But then—something shifted.

She stopped folding.

She sat down right there on the hallway floor, laundry still in her lap. And for the first time in a long time, she didn't rush through it. She didn't numb it. She didn't push past it. She breathed.

And in that breath, she didn't feel bitter. She felt still. She felt herself.

Because in that quiet moment, what shifted wasn't the laundry—it was *her relationship with herself.*

She stopped measuring her worth by what she could finish and started anchoring it in how gently she could *be*. She finally gave herself permission to *belong to herself* again and paused the pattern of leaving herself behind.

She told me, "It was the weirdest thing. The laundry wasn't done. I still had ten other things I could've been doing, but for once, I wasn't trying to outrun myself... I was just... there. With me."

It wasn't peace because everything was perfect.

It was peace because she chose to stop abandoning herself in the name of getting it all done.

That moment wasn't loud or theatrical. It didn't involve a journal, a self-care checklist, or a big emotional release.

It was just a moment of quiet permission.

A soft return to the woman buried underneath the doing.

And she realized: *this is what coming home feels like.*
Not a finish line. Not a version of her that finally had it all together.

But a version of her that was honest, steady, and rooted in something real.

She said, "I didn't need anyone to see me to feel seen. I just needed to stop long enough to see myself."

And that change was everything she needed.

And like the mama in the story, you, too, have made it. Not to perfection, but to presence. Not to the end, but to your center.

This is what it means to mother from the middle.

Not from the chaos of yesterday or the pressure of tomorrow. But from the steady space inside you—the space you've been coming back to, breath by breath, boundary by powerful boundary.

This chapter isn't a finish line. It's your homecoming.

Not an arrival into a new identity, but a remembering of the woman you were always becoming.

You are no longer surviving motherhood. You are leading it. You are no longer chasing calm. You are becoming it.

You are not parenting from the wounds of the past or the panic of the moment.

You're parenting from your middle. From your wisdom. From your wholeness. From your heart.

And that changes everything.

So sit back…breathe it in… and take your time with this major win as you reflect on how far you've bravely come and how intentionally, steadily, and faithfully you continue to go.

It's 7:43 a.m.

The cereal's on the floor. One child is sobbing over missing socks. The other just remembered a forgotten homework packet. Your partner can't find their keys. The dog is barking. Your phone is buzzing with an "urgent" email.

It's a scene you know well.

And just a few months ago, this moment might have undone you.

You would have clenched. Snapped. Spiraled. Fell apart.

You would have said something you didn't mean or shut down completely.

Because when you're mothering from the edge, even a teaspoon of chaos can feel like a tidal wave.

But today, you are doing something different.

You pause. You breathe. You place a hand over your heart and whisper:

"I am the center. Not the storm."

And it's not magic. The socks are still lost. The email still needs answering. The tantrum hasn't disappeared.

But *you* have changed.

Because you're not parenting from urgency—you're parenting from intention. You're not reacting—you're responding. Not with a lecture. Not with panic.

And in that one simple moment, your children learn what it means to find calm in chaos. To return to themselves. To lead with grace and have a safe place to land.

That's legacy... and more than that, that's what coming home feels like.

The woman who began this journey didn't need fixing. She needed support. She didn't need a makeover—she needed a mirror. A space to see herself more clearly. A place to remember what had always been true underneath the noise.

She came to this work carrying so much. Expectations. Exhaustion. Guilt.

Old scripts she never signed up for but found herself reciting anyway.

Realizing the hard truth that she was not the center of her life.

She showed up even when it felt heavy. Even when she wasn't sure it would work. Even when her days were loud and her nights were long.

And slowly—sometimes in barely noticeable ways—she started to soften.

Not into weakness, but into wisdom. Not into someone new, but into someone real.

You didn't just learn how to take a breath before yelling.

You didn't just pick up tools to de-escalate a meltdown. You reclaimed something.

There came a moment when you no longer measured your worth by how well you kept it all together. You began to trust that your presence—messy, tender, fully human—was enough. And in that shift, something sacred opened. You began leading from intention instead of instinct. You began feeling like *you* in your parenting, not just a referee, fixer, or ticking time bomb.

And while that shift is powerful, it can also come with pressure—the belief that healing means we never fall short again.

There's a mom I once worked with who believed healing meant never messing up again. That true growth looked like speaking in soft tones, keeping her cool in every conflict, and gliding through parenthood without ever losing her cool.

But what she learned instead is something I hope you never forget:

Healing is not about becoming someone else. It's about becoming someone who comes back.

After the raised voice. After the shut door. After the moment when your nervous system screamed louder than your values.

She told me, "I didn't have to be perfect—just available. And God met me there."

That's what coming home feels like.

Not that the house is always quiet, but that *you* are steady in the noise.

Not that the tears stop, but that you can be open when they fall.

Not that the chaos disappears, but that you remember who you are in the middle of it.

There was a time when it took everything you had to pause. When saying "let's reset" felt awkward. When boundaries felt like betrayal. When self-compassion sounded foreign, but not anymore.

Now, those practices aren't things you have to remember—they're things you *embody*.

They're not tools you pick up occasionally. They're a rhythm. A language. A presence.

That's what integration looks like.

You've interrupted the spiral more times than you can count. You've sat with guilt instead of running from it. You've repaired with tenderness instead of shame.

You've practiced—and now, you're living it. You're mothering from your middle.

From between generations. Between stimulus and response. From the wisdom that lives in your body, not just your brain.

This is what wholeness looks like. Not polished or perfect, but rooted.

You're not parenting from exhaustion. You're parenting from embodiment.

You're not using the R.I.S.E. Method as a script. You've allowed it to become your rhythm.

The calm you feel now—it didn't arrive overnight. It was built, breath by breath and moment by moment.

Through reflection, you honored your pain without letting it define you. Your past, your patterns—you stopped moving on autopilot and began noticing what shaped you, what triggered you, and what still lived in your body.

Through interruption, you disrupted the legacy you didn't choose. The old scripts, the inherited reactions, the shoulds and the shame. You built a pause into the moments that used to spiral.

Through shifting, you began to respond with your values instead of your wounds. You chose connection over control, boundaries over burnout.

And now, you embody your motherhood, not as a performance, but as a practice. This is where it all lives. Not in your notes. Not in your journal. But in your breath. In your tone. In your rituals. In your return.

You've stopped parenting from a place of reaction and started leading from intention.

This isn't about never falling apart. It's about knowing how to come back together.

You no longer live on the edge of breakdowns—you lead from the core of your being. You no longer fear the mess—you meet it with open arms.

Because you know something sacred now: The center is always here. And you can return to it—every single time.

If you're waiting to feel "done," release that now. There's no graduation here. No, "I've finally arrived."

This work—the kind of work that rewires legacies, that heals childhood echoes, that transforms daily rhythms—it doesn't end.

But that shouldn't be discouraging; that's *liberating*.

Because you no longer need to strive for arrival. You just need to return.

To breath and pause. To softness and clarity. To the grounded truth that you don't have to be perfect to be powerful.

You don't have to know everything to lead with wisdom.

Will you still get triggered? Yes.

Will old patterns visit you from time to time? Of course.

Will you raise your voice, shut down, or lose it in the car? Most likely.

But now?

Now you *notice* sooner. You *repair* faster. You *return* more easily.

Because you're not lost anymore, you're rooted in *your* truth and purpose. You've been building muscle memory for calm. A nervous system and heart that can now say, "This is familiar. I know the way back."

That's what healing looks like. You'll come home again and again---not because you never wander, but because you now know the way.

To further manifest this incredible shift you now embody, celebrate becoming the you that has been waiting for your arrival by writing to the version of you who started this journey. The one who felt overwhelmed, unsure, and ashamed.

Tell her:

"You did it. You didn't need to become someone else. You needed to come home to yourself. And you did."

Then write to your future version for the next hard moment.

Remind her:

"You don't have to hustle for peace. It's already inside of you. The center is always here. You can return whenever you choose."

It's time to claim this version of you. The one who mothers from wholeness, not from wounds.

Light a candle. Sit with your journal. And write your truth.

"Coming home feels like..."

What does it feel like in your breath? Your body? Your parenting?

Then declare it, name it, and anchor into it.

And as you do, feel free to borrow from these affirmations—or write your own that inspires you:

- "I am a cycle-breaker, not a fixer."
- "I mother from love, not fear."
- "I give my children the emotional safety I longed for—and I give it to myself too."
- "I am not perfect. I am present. I am home."
- "The calm I was chasing now lives inside me."

Read it when the chaos is loud. Return to it when you forget. Let it be your emotional compass.

This identity you now embody no longer reaches for reactivity but speaks from a steady place—the kind only healing can build.

You're not just coping, you're leading. You're not just surviving motherhood but mothering with intention and purpose.

From the core of who you are, not who you were taught to be.

You mother from a place of wholeness—aware, anchored, and attuned.

As we draw to a close, ask yourself and reflect on:

- **What part of me feels more whole now than when I began this journey?**

- **How will I keep returning to her—day by day, breath by breath?**

Because this is not the end. It's the embodiment. The integration. The return.

You are not the chaos. You are not the shame. You are not the story that was passed down to you.

You are the center. You are the calm. This is who you are now.

And this is what coming home feels like. Welcome back, mama.

CONCLUSION

You've made it.

Not to some tidy finish line—because healing isn't linear, but to something far more powerful: a deeper, softer, wiser understanding of yourself.

You've unearthed patterns that were never yours to carry. You've paused long enough to hear the quiet truths beneath your reactions.

You've replaced shame with grace. Urgency with presence. Performance with permission. You've begun mothering—not from your edge, but from your middle.

This journey hasn't asked you to become someone new. It's helped you remember who you've always been beneath the noise: Calm, clear, connected, and capable.

You are no longer parenting from the edge of burnout or buried wounds.

You're no longer contorting yourself to meet old definitions of a "good mom."

You're no longer waiting for permission to feel peace.

You are leading now and anchoring into the emotional home your children can return to—not because everything is perfect, but because it's safe.

That doesn't mean the hard days are gone. But it means you'll meet them with gentler hands when they arrive. It doesn't mean you'll never mess up, but now, you'll know how to repair, with your children and yourself.

That is the mark of a conscious mother. Not control, but emotional clarity. Not perfection, but presence. Not survival, but self-trust.

And here's what I need you to remember, deep in your heart and spirit:

You are not too late. You are not too far off track. You are not too far gone to be restored.

You are becoming, in the most beautiful and brave way.

Because here's the truth: this wasn't a quick fix, and it wasn't about checking boxes or getting it "right."

This was about coming home to yourself.

Along the way, you've:

- Reflected on the stories that shaped you—and reclaimed the truth beneath them.
- Interrupted old patterns with awareness and compassion.
- Shifted from reactivity to intention, from fear to connection.
- Embodied a new legacy—not by being perfect, but by being present.

You've seen the ghosts. You've named the roles. You've laid down the weight of generational expectations. And more importantly, you've started rewriting the story.

Every time you whispered, *"I don't have to be who I had to be,"* You loosened the grip of the past.

Every time you choose repair over retreat, grace over shame, boundaries over burnout, you light a new path—not just for your children, but for yourself.

This is not the end of your journey but it is a sacred milestone worth honoring.

Because now, when the fear says, "You're failing," you'll pause instead of spiral.

Now, when the guilt rises, you'll meet it with curiosity, not collapse.

Now, when the old patterns call your name, you'll remember: *You have a choice.*

And every time you return to center—even imperfectly—you are breaking the cycle. Not by force, but by essence. By being. By choosing to mother from your wholeness, not your wounds.

Your children won't remember every rule you kept or every mess you cleaned, but they will remember how it felt to be loved by you.

And now?

They'll remember safety. They'll remember softness. They'll remember a mother who tried. Who paused. Who stayed. Who showed them that love lives in the hard moments, too.

This isn't just a parenting shift. It's a generational shift.

And you did it.

One breath, one return, and one brave decision at a time.

You already are the legacy.

So, take a breath, place a hand on your heart, and let this truth settle in you:

You are the mother your children will remember and the woman you were always meant to come home to.

This is what healing looks like. This is what wholeness feels like. This is who you are *now*.

You've arrived.

NEXT STEPS

You've done something remarkable. You didn't just read this book—you lived it. You reflected, paused, softened, and shifted. You showed up for your healing and your legacy.

And this is just the beginning.

If your heart is stirring with the question: "What now?"

I want to invite you to take the next step with me inside my live workshop:

Break the Cycle Insider,

An immersive, soul-shifting experience for intentional mothers ready to take their healing deeper—designed not just to inspire, but to equip you with a tangible, take-it-with-you practice to regulate, reconnect, and reset the moment life feels heavy.

In this intimate and powerful workshop, I'll walk you through how I used the exact R.I.S.E. Method along with my P.E.A.C.E. Framework in my own life—not just in theory, but in real, messy, motherhood moments—to break cycles, reclaim my identity, and create emotional safety that my children could feel.

Think of RISE as the *arc* of transformation.

Each stage is supported by the tools inside my PEACE Framework — so mom, you aren't just learning ideas, you're *moving through real shifts.*

I'll share the behind-the-scenes stories:

- The patterns I had to unlearn to stop yelling and start connecting
- The guilt that used to derail me—and how I learned to rise from it
- The small, sacred rituals that became anchors in my motherhood

And most importantly, I'll guide you to begin applying this in your own story.

Inside the Break the Cycle Insider Workshop, You'll Learn:

1. The 3 most common blocks cycle-breakers face when trying to "do it differently"—and how to move through them with compassion.
2. Why information alone doesn't lead to transformation—and how embodiment creates lasting change
3. How to use the R.I.S.E. Method and P.E.A.C.E Framework beyond the page—and actually live it in your parenting, partnerships, and self-care.
4. What's really keeping you stuck in old responses—and how to begin responding from your center, not your past.

This isn't another workshop that tells you to "just stay calm."

It's a sacred space to remember who you are, be witnessed in your growth, and receive the next-level tools that help you integrate everything you've begun in this book.

You'll leave this workshop with:

- Deeper clarity about what's next on your healing path.
- A personal blueprint to continue breaking cycles with intention.
- A powerful invitation into my full program—where we take this work even deeper, together.

You've started the journey. Let me walk with you a little further.

Click here to save your spot inside Break the Cycle Insider →
https://nurturedconnect.kartra.com/page/workshop

Because you don't have to do this alone anymore. Your next breakthrough is already waiting.

Can't wait to see you there!

ABOUT THE AUTHOR

Alicia Brown is a Licensed Marriage & Family Therapist, Parent Educator, and the founder of *Mom-ing with Intent*, a movement rooted in helping mothers to heal what they've inherited—without losing who they are. Through her compassionate, faith-informed approach, Alicia has become a trusted guide for women who are ready to lead their families with emotional clarity, deep connection, and grace.

With over a decade of experience and a heart for cycle-breaking moms, Alicia combines clinical insight, lived experience, and soul-centered wisdom to help women move from survival mode to anchored, intentional leadership in their homes. Her signature R.I.S.E. and P.E.A.C.E. methods have transformed the lives of countless families and are woven throughout this book as a path back to self, purpose, and peaceful parenting.

A devoted wife and mother of three daughters, Alicia is passionate about building a legacy through love, not fear. Whether she's supporting families, leading workshops, or whispering encouragement through the pages of this book, Alicia's mission remains the same: to help women heal forward, parent with purpose, and raise emotionally rooted children who don't have to recover from their childhoods.

Connect with Alicia:

Instagram: @thealiciabrown

Facebook: Alicia P. Brown, LMFT

YouTube: @thealiciabrown

www.ingramcontent.com/pod-product-compliance
Lightning Source LLC
Chambersburg PA
CBHW050913160426
43194CB00011B/2392